THE DICTATOR POPE

THE DICTATOR POPE

The Inside Story of the Francis Papacy

Completely Revised and Updated

REGNERY
PUBLISHING
A Division of Salem Media Group

Cataloging-in-Publication data on file with the Library of Congress

ISBN 978-1-62157-832-1
e-book ISBN 978-1-62157-833-8

Published in the United States by
Regnery Publishing
A Division of Salem Media Group
300 New Jersey Ave NW
Washington, DC 20001
www.Regnery.com

Manufactured in the United States of America

10 9 8 7 6 5 4 3 2 1

Books are available in quantity for promotional or premium use. For information on discounts and terms, please visit our website: www.Regnery.com.

"You can fool all the people some of the time, and some of the people all the time, but you cannot fool all the people all the time."
—attributed to Abraham Lincoln

CONTENTS

Chapter 1

THE ST. GALLEN MAFIA

The Pope of Surprises

If you speak to the Catholics of Buenos Aires, they will tell you of the miraculous change that has taken over Jorge Mario Bergoglio. Their dour, unsmiling archbishop was turned overnight into the smiling, jolly Pope Francis, the idol of the people with whom he so fully identifies. If you speak to anyone working in the Vatican, they will tell you about the miracle in reverse. When the publicity cameras are off him, Pope Francis turns into a different figure: arrogant, dismissive of people, prodigal with bad language, and notorious for furious outbursts of temper which are known to everyone from the cardinals to the chauffeurs.

As Pope Francis said himself on the evening of his election, the cardinals in the Conclave of March 2013 seemed to have decided to go "to the ends of the Earth" to choose their pope, but the realization is now dawning that they had not troubled to check their merchandise. At first, he seemed a breath of fresh air, his rejections of convention being the signs of a man who was going to bring bold, radical reform into the Church. After five years of his pontificate, it is becoming increasingly clear that the reform is not being delivered. Instead, what we have is a revolution in personal style, but a revolution which is not a happy one for what Catholics consider the most sacred office on Earth. Conservative Catholics are worried at the changes in moral teaching that Francis seems to be introducing, while liberals are dissatisfied because those changes are vaguely expressed and do not go far enough. Over and above such fears, however, are faults that ought to move all Catholics concerned for the integrity of the Church and the papal office. After five years of his pontificate, Francis is showing that he is not the democratic, liberal ruler that the cardinals thought they were electing in 2103, but a papal tyrant the like of whom has not been seen for many centuries. Shocking as the accusation may be, it is backed up by incontrovertible evidence. This book traces the failed reforms which have falsified the hopes that were placed in Francis, and describes in detail the reign of fear in the Vatican which the pope from Argentina has introduced.

After five years of Pope Francis Bergoglio, it is being said with more frequency, and more openly, that the strange situation in today's Vatican resembles nothing less than a Dan Brown potboiler novel, complete with conspiracies of eminent churchmen, sexual and financial scandals, and shady international banking interests. While many look hopefully to Pope Francis to relax the Church's traditional doctrines and practices, there has been surprisingly little attention paid to a remark by one of the highest ranking and most powerful prelates in the western world, that he was elected by a liberal "mafia," a group of progressive bishops and cardinals who had worked for years to bring about exactly this end.

Far from being an accusation from Church conservatives, the term was first used in a television interview[1] in September 2015 by Cardinal Godfried Danneels, the retired but still hugely influential archbishop of Mechelen-Brussels. Danneels said that he had for years been part of this group that had opposed Pope Benedict XVI throughout his reign. The group had, he said, worked to bring about a "much more modern" Catholic Church, and the election of the archbishop of Buenos Aires, Jorge Mario Bergoglio, as pope. An examination of the background of these extraordinary comments can give an insight into the nature of current ecclesiastical politics, particularly in liberal European episcopal circles.

"The St. Gallen group is sort of a posh name," Danneels said, to appreciative laughs from a live audience. "But in reality we called ourselves and that group: 'the mafia.'" The cardinal was speaking on a Belgian television program. In the brief video uploaded to the internet containing Danneels's remarks, a voice-over summarized the nature of the group that "met every year since 1996" in St. Gallen, Switzerland, originally at the invitation of the town's bishop, Ivo Fürer, and the famous Italian Jesuit and academic, and archbishop of Milan, Cardinal Carlo Maria Martini.

"Together they organised the secret 'resistance' against Cardinal Ratzinger, who at that time was the right-hand man of John Paul II," as head of the Congregation for the Doctrine of the Faith.

"When Pope John Paul II died in 2005, the group already pushed the present pope [Francis] to the fore," though this first attempt failed to put Jorge Mario Bergoglio on the throne. When faced with the election of Ratzinger as Pope Benedict XVI, "Danneels could hardly hide his disappointment," the narrator says.

Danneels gave the interview to promote his authorized biography, and added that the St. Gallen Group had bishops and cardinals, "too many to name." But all of them held the same general aim: the implementation of a "liberal/progressivist" agenda, and opposition to Pope Benedict and the direction of moderate doctrinal conservatism. Although later it was denied that the group was secret, Danneels said, "Things were discussed very freely; no reports were made so that everyone could blow off steam."

The program interviewed one of Danneels's biographers, Jürgen Mettepenningen (who co-authored the authorized biography with Karim Schelkens), saying that by 2013, with the resignation of Benedict, "You can say that through his participation in that group, Cardinal Danneels has been one of those who were the pioneers of the choice of Pope Francis."

The authors of the Danneels biography listed the group's concerns as "the situation of the Church," the "primacy of the Pope," "collegiality," and "John Paul II's succession." English Vaticanist Edward Pentin writes that they "also discussed centralism in the Church, the function of bishops' conferences, development of the priesthood, sexual morality, [and] the appointment of bishops," a schema more or less identical to the one that was to come into public view at the two Synods on the Family convened by Pope Francis in 2014 and 2015.

As one of the most powerful Catholic prelates in Europe and one of the leading voices in the dominant liberal camp of the European episcopate, Danneels's biography was of great public interest. Lest it be imagined that the cardinal was joking, the existence and general purpose of the St. Gallen "mafia" was confirmed the next day by biographer Karim Schelkens in an interview with a local St. Gallen radio station.[2] Edward Pentin summarized what was known about the group, writing in the *National Catholic Register*: "The personalities and theological ideas of the members sometimes differed, but one thing united them: their dislike of the then-prefect of the Congregation for the Doctrine of the Faith, Cardinal Joseph Ratzinger." Pentin continued, "The group wanted a drastic reform of the Church, much more modern and current, with Jorge Bergoglio, Pope Francis, as its head. They got what they wanted." Pentin added in a later article that although the St. Gallen Group officially ceased meeting in 2006, there can be no doubt that its influence continued into 2013. "It's safe to say that it helped form a network that paved the way for at least favoring Cardinal Bergoglio at the Conclave seven years later."[3]

In 2015,[4] the German author and Vatican expert Paul Badde confirmed this, saying[5] that he had received "reliable information" that three days after the burial of Pope John Paul II, Cardinals Martini, Lehmann, and Kasper from Germany, Backis from Lithuania, van Luyn from the Netherlands, Danneels from Brussels, and Murphy-O'Connor from London "met in the so-called Villa Nazareth in Rome, the home of Cardinal Silvestrini who was then no longer eligible to vote; they then discussed in secret a tactic of how to avoid the election of Joseph Ratzinger."

Following the revelations by Danneels, a somewhat confused letter[6] appeared from the diocese of St. Gallen that partially retracted the claim that the group had influenced the resignation of Pope Benedict. The letter did confirm that the election of Jorge Bergoglio as Pope Francis in 2013 "corresponded to the goal pursued in St. Gallen," noting that this information came from Cardinal Danneels's biography. "This is confirmed by Bishop Ivo Fürer," the letter continued, who said that his "joy at the choice of the Argentinian was never made a secret."

Danneels's biography says that the group started forming well before 1996. In 1982, Danneels attended meetings of the Council of the European Bishops' Conferences (CCEE) for the first time and met Martini and Ivo Fürer, who is described as "the zealous and discreet secretary of CCEE." Martini took the reins of the CCEE in 1987; his leadership was decidedly in the liberal direction, and by 1993 Pope John Paul II had decided that the group's secretary was to be a bishop appointed by Rome, that Curial prelates should attend the meetings, and that the venue should be moved to Rome.

In 1993 the pope transferred CCEE presidency from Martini's hands into those of Miloslav Vlk, the archbishop of Prague. It is possible this was prompted by the fall of the Berlin Wall and the collapse of the Soviet Union, with the desirability of involving Eastern European bishops. Vlk would have been unlikely to be interested in the type of reform dear to the hearts of Martini and Hume.

These changes hampered the CCEE as a vehicle for liberal pressure on the Church and it was from this period that Danneels disengaged himself from it. The St. Gallen Group began meeting in 1996 at the invitation of Ivo Fürer—who had been appointed bishop of St. Gallen in 1995—three years after this change of management.

Later, the two Danneels biographers partly retracted their description of the St. Gallen Group as a liberal "lobby" group. But even so the same ambiguity could be detected as in the letter from the St. Gallen diocese which they quoted in their statements. Pentin reported[7] on September 26, 2015, that the biographers repeated the official letter from the diocese, saying the "election of Bergoglio corresponded with the aims of St. Gallen; on that there is no doubt. And the outline of its programme was that of Danneels and his confreres who had been discussing it for ten years." They said the failure to elect Bergoglio in 2005 led to the disbanding of the group. Pentin points out, however, that some of St. Gallen's members or their close associates were later named by the English papal biographer Austen Ivereigh, as part of "Team Bergoglio," the group of cardinals who finally brought the St. Gallen plan to fruition at the Conclave of 2013.

The prelates in the group had been most concerned with preventing Ratzinger's election at the Conclave in 2005. But more generally it is not difficult to determine from examining their careers in which direction the members of the St. Gallen "mafia" hoped to steer the Church. The idea was simple; to gather these powerful, like-minded prelates together to use their vast networks of contacts to bring about what political analysts would recognize as "regime change."

The program they were advancing was couched in the watchwords of "decentralization," "collegiality," and a more "pastoral" Church. By the last term they meant that they wanted to get away from the firm upholding of Catholic moral teaching that had characterized Pope John Paul II and move towards the approach that has since been seen in the Synod on the Family.[8] The slogans of decentralization and collegiality are also an implicit criticism of John Paul II and of the way he governed the Church. John Paul came to the throne after the fifteen-year reign of Paul VI, in whose time the radical consequences of the Second Vatican Council were worked out. Whether Paul VI's liberal interpretation of the Council was the right one is nowadays a subject of controversy (it has been challenged by the "Hermeneutic of Continuity" argued by Benedict XVI); but what cannot be disputed was that the results of Paul VI's government were in some areas unfortunate. Nearly fifty thousand priests abandoned the priesthood during these years, vocations to the religious life in general, among both men and women, suffered a collapse of similar scale, and there was a widespread rejection of Church teaching—not least of Paul VI's own encyclical *Humanae vitae*.

The phenomenon was accentuated by Paul VI's appointments to the episcopate. To take one example from the United States, the hierarchy there was transformed by the nominations made by the nuncio Archbishop Jadot, who in a brief seven years (1973–1980) managed to appoint 103 bishops and promote fifteen archbishops. Among the latter, nominees who proved especially scandalous included Archbishop Hunthausen of Seattle, whose management later provoked Vatican intervention and the imposition of a coadjutor, and above all Archbishop Weakland of Milwaukee, who eventually resigned after he had paid $450,000 from diocesan funds to a male lover who was threatening him with a lawsuit. Such consequences of advancing "liberal" pastors were felt in greater or lesser degree in many sectors of the worldwide Church.

John Paul II came to the papal throne with a determination to stop the rot, and to a large extent he succeeded, but he left many discontents among those who were of Paul VI's school. Since John Paul could often not rely on the hierarchy he had been bequeathed, he followed a policy of greater papal control as the only viable option to restore orthodox teaching and Catholic religious life. Undoubtedly, he tightened up Church discipline, but whether he can fairly be called a "centralizer," who was not "collegial" in spirit, is open to question. John Paul II's centralism, against which the prelates of the St. Gallen Group professed to be reacting, was a response to a state of chaos which had come in by equally centralist means. It would be naïve not to recognize that the slogans of decentralization and collegiality used by the Group were code words for a broad liberal program, which needs to be described.

Those who have watched the Catholic scene over the last thirty years would readily recognize the names of the leading figures of the St. Gallen Group. Among those listed by Pentin, the most famous are Danneels, with the bible scholar and *papabile* archbishop of Milan Cardinal Carlo Maria Martini, and the German theologian Cardinal Walter Kasper.

Martini

The most illustrious of the St. Gallen names and its indisputable leader was Cardinal Carlo Maria Martini, for most of the years of both John Paul II and Benedict XVI considered the leading figure of the Church's liberal faction. A reading of Martini's interviews and writings gives a hint as to Bergoglio's enthusiasm for his declared mentor; many of the cardinal's favorite terms and phrases reappear in Pope Francis own writing and off-the-cuff speeches.

In 2008, Sandro Magister described Cardinal Martini as habitually "subtle and opaque," but added there were times he came out into the open; one could easily tell where he stood (on the "progressive" side of issues) while for form's sake he remained vague. "About priestly celibacy, for example, he says and doesn't say. The same about women priests. And about homosexuality. And contraception. And when he criticizes the Church hierarchy, he doesn't give names, of persons or things." [9]

But that year, Martini gave a book-length interview[10] in which he openly challenged the teaching of Pope Paul VI on contraception in *Humanae vitae*. The controverted encyclical's prohibition of contraception, the cardinal said, has caused "serious damage," and he blamed it for the abandonment of the practice of the faith by many Catholics since 1968.

The cardinal particularly praised the responses to the encyclical of the Austrian, German, and other national bishops' conferences, saying they "followed a path along which we can continue today." This "new culture of tenderness" is "an approach to sexuality that is more free from prejudice."

In contrast, John Paul II had "followed the path of rigorous application" of *Humanae vitae*. "He didn't want there to be any doubts on this point. It seems that he even considered a declaration that would enjoy the privilege of papal infallibility."

"I am firmly convinced that the Church can point out a better way than it did with *Humanae vitae*," Martini said. "Being able to admit one's mistakes and the limitations of one's previous viewpoints is a sign of greatness of soul and of confidence. The Church would regain credibility and competence."[11]

Martini, who died in 2012 only months before Pope Benedict announced his resignation, was an Italian Jesuit, a renowned biblical scholar. He served as archbishop of Milan through the most productive years of John Paul II's reign, 1980 to 2002. As the most influential figure in the Italian Catholic Church, and as head of the archdiocese of Milan—traditionally a strong *"papabile"* see—Martini was long considered the ideal liberal candidate for the papacy. He fell out of the running, however, after a diagnosis of a rare form of Parkinson's disease. He resigned his see in 2002, but remained the most important figure on the Church's Left in Europe.

Only hours after his death in August 2012, *Corriere della Sera* published a last interview. Almost with his dying breath Martini maintained that the Church as an institution is "200 years out of date." The cardinal said, "The Church must recognize its mistakes and must take a radical path of change, starting with the Pope and the bishops." This was to be particularly in the area of sexual teachings that, he implied, were the cause of the clerical sex-abuse crisis. In the interview, Martini mapped out the policies which were to be put forward by the liberals in the two Synods on the Family in 2014 and 2015, and which were later incorporated, in a more ambiguous fashion, in Pope Francis's exhortation *Amoris laetitia*: he urged a more personal and less doctrinal approach to sexual morality, appealed especially to the case of divorced and remarried couples, who he declared "need special protection," and expressed dissent from the Church's traditional attitude toward homosexuality.[12]

Kasper

While Martini was mainly known within Italy, the German Walter Kasper has a higher profile in North America, where he has regularly lectured and given interviews. Kasper's books have been translated into English and published in the United States for decades, and he has been a visiting professor at the Catholic University of America since 1983. But it is as the man who launched the most furious controversy of Pope Francis's pontificate that his name will likely live after him.

Pope Francis invited Kasper to give the keynote address at the consistory of February 2014, sparking a chain of events and a storm of debate that has only grown. It was at this consistory that he presented the "Kasper Proposal"—that divorced and civilly remarried Catholics could be allowed to receive absolution and Communion after following a "penitential process," but without the need of a promise to abstain from marital relations. But this pinnacle of Kasper's career follows decades of pressing in every available venue for what can arguably be described as the Martini Agenda.

Kasper steadily and publicly opposed Pope John Paul II and Pope Benedict XVI, even while serving as a Curial official. For most of the reign of John Paul II, and earlier as a student and assistant to the radical theologian Fr. Hans Küng at the University of Tübingen, Kasper's name was synonymous with the progressivist camp in Germany and in the Curia. Pressing for acceptance of his proposal for divorced and remarried Catholics has become the core of Kasper's public work in recent years, but it was not until the election of Jorge Bergoglio as pope that the goal seemed possible.

In his very first Sunday Angelus address, March 17, 2013, the new pope gave what was perhaps his most obvious signal of the direction he intended to take. Speaking of Kasper's new book, *Mercy: The Essence of the Gospel and the Key to Christian Life*, Francis said, "In the past few days I have been reading a book by a Cardinal—Cardinal Kasper, a clever theologian, a good theologian—on mercy. And that book did me a lot of good, but do not think I am promoting my cardinals' books! Not at all! Yet it has done me so much good, so much good.... Cardinal Kasper said that feeling mercy, that this word changes everything."[13]

At a talk at Fordham University, Kasper related the story of "an old cardinal" who after this address had tried to warn the pope that "there are heresies in this book." The new pope, Kasper said, recounted the story back to him, and smiled, adding the reassurance, "This enters in one ear and goes out the other."[14]

In an interview with *Commonweal*, Kasper outlined his position, saying he was opposed to the "rigorist" approach of moral theology of the past. He took the logic a step further, saying that a divorced and remarried Catholic was morally obliged not to give up the new relationship. Repentance in the traditional Catholic sense is sometimes impossible, and even potentially sinful. People "must do the best possible in a given situation," and if there were children from the second marriage a couple who observed the traditional Catholic requirement would incur active guilt by breaking up the second family.[15]

With the Synods on the Family looming, Kasper became even more outspoken at a book launch in Rome, adopting one of the slogans of the LGBT lobby, that homosexuality should not be made subject to "fundamentalism."

"For me, this inclination is a question mark: it does not reflect the original design of God and yet it is a reality, because you are born gay."[16]

Danneels

Certainly, among the most high-profile of these churchmen is Godfried Danneels himself, for more than thirty years the head not only of the wealthy and influential Brussels archdiocese, but of a network of political, social, and judicial contacts that gave him immense political influence. In his long tenure, Danneels never troubled to hold back on his opinions on most of the "hot-button" issues of concern to the Church, particularly in the areas of sexual morality, abortion, contraception, homosexuality, and homosexual marriage.

Danneels was well known throughout Europe for his wielding of political clout to press for liberalization of Belgium's laws regarding sex and marriage. In 1990, he advised King Baudouin of Belgium to sign a law legalizing abortion and later refused to withdraw explicit sex education materials—condemned as pornographic by many parents—from Belgian Catholic schools. He was on record saying that Belgium's legalization of same-sex marriage was a "positive development."[17] In May 2003, he wrote to Prime Minister Guy Verhofstadt, congratulating Verhofstadt's government on "the approval of a legal statute for a stable relationship between partners of the same sex."

A few months after his retirement, in April 2010, Danneels was especially under a cloud of scandal, being accused of having covered for a protégé bishop who admitted to having sexually abused a minor, his own nephew. In 2010[18] it was revealed—by the publication of an audio recording—that Danneels had told the victim to keep quiet and not cause trouble for the soon-to-retire Bishop Roger Vangheluwe of Bruges, even suggesting that the victim ought to "ask forgiveness." Before the recordings were released, Danneels had denied all knowledge of sexual abuse by clergy or cover-ups. But a whistleblowing priest, Rik Devillé, later claimed that he had warned Danneels about Vangheluwe in the mid-1990s.[19] Because the legal statute of limitations had expired, Vangheluwe was never charged for his crimes, though he issued public apologies to the victims.

Following this, a wave of complaints of hundreds of cases of sexual abuse by clerics over a twenty-year period prompted an intervention by police who raided Danneels's house and the diocesan offices. Computers and files were seized,[20] including all the documentation gathered by the diocesan commission on the abuse allegations. The cardinal was later questioned by prosecutors for ten hours but no charges were laid.

For reasons that remain unclear, the seized evidence was declared to have been inadmissible, the documents returned to the archdiocese and the investigation was abruptly closed. This despite the fact that individuals had come forward with almost five hundred separate complaints, including many that alleged

Danneels had used his power and connections to shield clerical sex abusers.

Peter Adriaenssens, the chairman of the sex abuse commission launched by Danneels's successor, Archbishop André-Joseph Léonard, complained to the prosecutors about the raids, saying the result was that his team had lost all 475 dossiers they had collected on abuse allegations. The commission was dissolved and no further investigations ever undertaken, despite Adriaenssens having said that about fifty of the dossiers implicated Danneels.

In December of the same year, Danneels stated to a parliamentary committee on sexual abuse that there had never been any policy of covering up for clerical abusers. The archdiocese of Mechelen-Brussels later issued a public apology for "silence" on clerical sexual abuse of minors.

Retirement proved a disappointment to Danneels, whose successor, a noted Ratzingerian conservative, he described as "totally unsuitable for Brussels." With the 2005 election of Joseph Ratzinger as Pope Benedict, Danneels's star seemed to have irredeemably faded.

But the 2013 Conclave returned him to the forefront of Church politics, with the new pope inviting him to join him on St. Peter's *loggia* for his first appearance to the crowds. He was given the privilege of intoning the formal prayers at Francis's inauguration Mass. Later, the cardinal, whom many had considered "disgraced," was invited by Pope Francis as a special papal favor to attend both Synods on the Family where he took a prominent role. Danneels himself described his last Conclave as "a personal resurrection experience."

"Team Bergoglio"

Despite the rules of strict secrecy, it was revealed after the 2005 Conclave that the obscure Jesuit archbishop of Buenos Aires, Jorge Mario Bergoglio, had been the runner-up.[21] The St. Gallen Group were nearly all present and working hard for their candidate. And their support was significant. On the penultimate ballot, Bergoglio had forty votes to Ratzinger's seventy-two. Paul Badde said that it was Cardinal Meisner of Cologne who had "passionately fought" the St. Gallen Group "and especially Cardinal Danneels," in favor of Ratzinger. An anonymous cardinal, who kept a diary of the proceedings, said that the group came close: "The Argentine Jesuit is a step away from the numerical threshold of 39 votes, which, theoretically, could allow an organized minority to block the election of any candidate." History shows the outcome. The St. Gallen Group retreated after 2005, but its defeat was temporary.

Benedict's pontificate was tumultuous, particularly in its last year, and with his surprise resignation, whether the group had a hand in it or not, the group saw a last-ditch opportunity. With Martini dead, and most of the group coming within a hair of the cutoff age for participation in a Conclave, time was running out—they knew this was their last realistic chance. With the "sede vacante" period that precedes a Conclave officially starting only days before Walter Kasper's eightieth birthday, some have asked if it was not too much to believe the timing of Benedict's sudden resignation was mere coincidence. Danneels's eightieth birthday was to come only a couple of months later, and Lehmann had only another three years.

The question of vote campaigning at a Conclave is crucial because the 1996 papal legal document governing Conclaves,

Universi Dominici gregis, specifically forbids this kind of activity and levels a penalty of automatic excommunication both for those who campaign and for the one who gives his consent to the campaigners.

Pope John Paul II held that a Conclave must be a religious, not a political event, and that cardinal electors must have recourse to prayer and the inspiration of the Holy Spirit, not worldly factionalism. Still less was there to be a cabal who intended to use a Conclave to steer the Church from behind the throne. As is stated unequivocally in *Universi Dominici gregis*, "Let the Cardinal electors, moreover, abstain from all pacts, agreements, promises and any other obligations, by which they might be constrained to give or refuse support for anyone."

Despite this reformist ambition, in his 2014 book on Bergoglio, *The Great Reformer*, Ivereigh wrote about the open vote campaigning that went on among a group of four cardinals in 2013. Three were St. Gallen alumni: Walter Kasper, Godfried Danneels, and Cardinal Karl Lehmann. Among them, however, was the heir to the group's English representative, Cardinal Basil Hume, archbishop of Westminster. Hume had died in 1999, but his ideological and episcopal successor was Cardinal Cormac Murphy-O'Connor. Ivereigh wrote that though he was over eighty it was Murphy-O'Connor's role during the pre-Conclave general congregations and social engagements to recruit the anglosphere voting cardinals to the cause.

Although Cardinal Bergoglio was not himself a member of the St. Gallen Group, Ivereigh said he nevertheless verbally gave his "assent" to Murphy-O'Connor to be a lobbyist for "Team Bergoglio," an action also forbidden by a strict interpretation of

Universi Dominici gregis. Although all four cardinals Ivereigh named later denied his claim—and Ivereigh pledged to edit future editions of the book—in the case at least of Cardinal Murphy-O'Connor his own prior statements contradict the denial. In late 2013, the archbishop of Westminster gave an interview to the *Catholic Herald* in which he admitted not only to campaigning at the Conclave but also to gaining Bergoglio's assent to do so.

The article by Miguel Cullen in the September 12, 2013, edition of the *Herald* says, "The cardinal also disclosed that he had spoken to the future Pope as they left the *Missa pro Eligendo Romano Pontifice*, the final Mass before the conclave began on March 12."

Murphy-O'Connor said, "We talked a little bit. I told him he had my prayers and said, in Italian: 'Be careful.' I was hinting, and he realized and said: 'Si–capisco'—yes, I understand. He was calm. He was aware that he was probably going to be a candidate going in. Did I know he was going to be Pope? No. There were other good candidates. But I knew he would be one of the leading ones.'"[22] The admonition to Bergoglio to "be careful" certainly seems to imply that Murphy-O'Connor—and Bergoglio—knew he was at least bending the rules.

This is supported again in the same article in the *Herald* where Murphy-O'Connor is quoted saying, "All the cardinals had a meeting with him in the Hall of Benedictions, two days after his election. We all went up one by one. He greeted me very warmly. He said something like: 'It's your fault. What have you done to me?'"[23]

In an interview with the *Independent* after the Conclave, Murphy-O'Connor also hinted there was a particular program laid before the seventy-six-year-old Argentinian that he was expected to accomplish in about four years. The English cardinal told journalist and author Paul Vallely, "Four years of Bergoglio would be enough to change things."[24] A fair enough comment after the fact, but this was the same phrase recorded by Andrea Tornielli in *La Stampa* in an article dated March 2, 2013, eleven days before Bergoglio's election: "'Four years of Bergoglio would be enough to change things,' whispers a cardinal and long-time friend of the archbishop of Buenos Aires."[25]

The situation was summarized recently by Matthew Schmitz writing in *First Things*, who said, "Though Benedict is still living, Francis is trying to bury him."[26]

Chapter 2

THE CARDINAL FROM ARGENTINA

When Cardinal Bergoglio was elected Pope Francis in 2013, he had been head of the Catholic Church in Argentina for fifteen years, and was nationally a very well-known figure. It would have been possible for the cardinals to obtain details on how he was seen on his home ground; but papal conclaves do not resemble an appointment to the post of CEO in a multi-national company, with references demanded of the candidates. Since his election, Pope Francis has taken the world by surprise, and that probably includes most of the cardinals who voted for him.

The purpose of this chapter is to look over the record of Bergoglio's earlier career and fill the gap that the cardinals neglected to scrutinize. The sources used begin with the full biography written by Austen Ivereigh, *The Great Reformer*, which is an outsider's account, and also, by no coincidence, the most hagiographical. Principally, however, the aim here is to summarize accounts by

Bergoglio's fellow countrymen, people who knew him well over many years and who knew the state of the Argentinian Church from the inside. They tell a story with which the rest of the world was notably unacquainted, but which goes a long way towards explaining Francis's style and policy as we have witnessed them for the last five years.

Jorge Mario Bergoglio was born on December 17, 1936, in a suburb of Buenos Aires, the son of a struggling accountant. The signs of strain that can be detected in his family are not merely economic. The adult Jorge was not given to speaking of his parents. After the birth of her fifth child, his mother became temporarily an invalid and had to delegate the upbringing of her children to a woman called Concepción. Jorge celebrated this surrogate as a good woman, yet he admitted that he treated her badly when, years later, she came to him to ask for his help as bishop in Buenos Aires and he sent her away, in his own words, "quickly and in a very bad way."[1] The incident seems to point to strains which are buried in the past but may provide a clue to Bergoglio's enigmatic personality.

On the sociological side, the times were difficult enough. Argentina had been hit by the worldwide economic depression of the 1930s and was suffering a reverse such as it had not known in living memory. In the half-century before the First World War, Argentina had been awash with British investment, was a major agricultural exporter, and became the eighth-richest country in the world. A last burst of prosperity came in the Second World War, when a beleaguered Britain was desperate for Argentinian meat exports. The wartime boom was followed by a peacetime economic collapse.

Politically, Argentina's dominant ideology in the twentieth century was Peronism, a sort of populist fascism based on the rule of Juan and Evita Perón. Juan Perón was president of Argentina from 1946 to 1955, between Jorge Bergoglio's tenth and nineteenth years, and the boy's outlook, like that of all of his generation, became riveted by this unique figure and the movement he founded. Perón's secret was to exploit the grievances of a *nouveau riche* society that had suddenly lost its bonanza. He championed the little man—a class to which the Bergoglio family undoubtedly belonged—against the plutocracy that had been exploiting him for so long; he used a nationalist and anti-foreign rhetoric, casting Argentina as a victim, as if the country had not been enriching itself for a lifetime on foreign demand for its exports. Perón's wife, Evita, an ex-actress with a taste for luxury but a hatred of the grand circles to which she was an outsider, incarnated the regime's flashy and strident style. Juan Perón's chief political trait was a cynical opportunism which helped him to make use of right-wing and left-wing support in succession. Starting as the champion of Argentina's Catholic identity, by the 1950s Perón had quarreled with the Church and was running one of the most anti-clerical regimes in the world. He was ousted by a military coup in 1955 and spent the next eighteen years in exile in Spain, leaving behind him a dazzled and disappointed generation. Among his followers was the young Jorge Bergoglio, and time would show just how much of a disciple he was of Perón's style.

After a Catholic education in Buenos Aires, Jorge Bergoglio decided at the age of twenty-one to become a Jesuit, and he entered the novitiate of the order in 1958. He was ordained as a priest in 1969 and completed the long Jesuit training two years later. After his election as pope, eulogistic accounts of his career appeared, but it is worth noticing—not by way of denigration but of character study—a couple of traits which are mentioned by his biographer Austen Ivereigh. In his first years, an ostentatious display of piety incurred criticism from Jorge Bergoglio's fellow novices; and later, when he was a master and prefect of discipline in a boys' school run by the order, he was known for his way of handing out harsh punishments with an angelic face.[2]

After 1963, a wave of politicization overtook the Jesuits, in Argentina as in the rest of the world, and the characteristic trend was to left-wing politics; Bergoglio's link however was with right-wing Peronism. In 1971, he was made master of novices of the Argentinian Province, and he combined this task with support for the Guardia de Hierro ("Iron Guard"), who at that time were working for the return of the exiled Perón. Austen Ivereigh describes this involvement euphemistically as "giving spiritual support" to the movement; it was in fact a good deal more, and it exemplifies the political interests that were to distinguish Bergoglio all his life. By most standards, it was an unusual way for the novice master of a religious order to spend his spare time.

Bergoglio as Jesuit Provincial

In July 1973, after two years as master of novices, Father Jorge Bergoglio was made superior of the Argentinian Province; he was thirty-six years old and had completed his training only two years before. The post of provincial is typically entrusted to priests who are in their fifties and have years in posts of authority behind them, and we should study what this exceptional appointment means. At the age of thirty-six, Jorge Bergoglio was a formidable figure, as he has remained ever since, and it is worth pausing to examine him. As pope, Jorge Bergoglio has made himself famous for his rejection of frills and by his identification with the poor, and there is no reason to regard these as superficial traits. Those who know him testify to his personal austerity and his attachment to poverty in his personal habits. It was left to an Argentinian observer, Omar Bello, to weigh this characteristic and to link it to one which has been less discussed: the pursuit of power.

Bello said of Bergoglio: "He preserves the wisdom of understanding that one reaches the heights by throwing ballast overboard, an obvious strategy which we seem to have forgotten."[3] And this is in fact a very Jesuit lesson. The great power that the Society has often acquired in history has not been reached by pursuing pomps and dignities. One thinks of the lesson given in South America itself, where the Jesuit missions among the Indians, known as Reductions, ranked at one time almost as independent states; yet they were ruled by ordinary priests, bearing only the title Father and wearing the simple Jesuit habit. Or, closer to Bergoglio's time, there was the example given by Father Vladimir Ledochówski, who was superior general from 1915 to 1942 and stamped his personality on the order. His career was a stellar one: provincial at thirty-six, assistant to the general at forty, and elected general himself at forty-eight. This beautifully mannered Polish aristocrat turned himself into a model of powerful austerity, a small, spare figure, with close-cropped hair, dressed in the plain black cassock, but directing an order that

grew from seventeen thousand to more than twenty-six thousand
members in his time, with a vast increase in its missionary work.
No Jesuit who entered the order in the middle of the twentieth
century would have been ignorant of that example.

The traditional Jesuit training is directed at producing men
whose self-discipline and discernment will make them effective
in their mission, following the guidelines laid down by St. Ignatius in the sixteenth century, and this in turn implies a scalpel-like
psychology. One does not want to fall into the cliché of depicting
the Society of Jesus as an especially Machiavellian body. That
accusation has been made against every order that tries to make
itself effective in the world, as it is today against Opus Dei. It is
true, however, that the methods of superiors, in an order famous
for its obedience, typically envisaged managing their subjects
somewhat as pawns, ideally for their own good. In the hands of
a wise superior such methods could be beneficial, but one can see
that they might also slip into psychological manipulation. If we
look at Father Jorge Bergoglio's record as master of novices, the
reports are that his methods of control were on the rough side,
and this impression is backed by the information given by Austen
Ivereigh. He notes that Bergoglio had three novices under him in
his first year and four in his second, but that by the time he took
over as Provincial in 1973 the Province had only two men left in
the novitiate; the implication is that, for whatever reason, he had
lost half of his novices.[4]

This would not have been very unusual, for in 1973 the Argentinian Province, like the whole Society of Jesus, was in a state of
crisis. Its general from 1965 to 1981 was the Spanish Father Pedro
Arrupe, who, after his election, felt obliged to follow the lead of

the major Jesuit intellectuals in interpreting the Second Vatican Council in an extremely liberal way. The result was that under his leadership, the Society collapsed from thirty-six thousand to twenty-six thousand members, wiping out the advance that the order had made since the Second World War. The characteristic novelty of the Jesuits' politicization in this period, especially in Latin America, was an embracing of the Marxist-inspired ideology of "liberation." By the early 1970s, the Jesuits' retreat from their older spiritual mission, the apparent relaxing of religious standards, and the pursuit of liberation theology had led to an exodus of its members, nowhere more so than in Argentina. Already in 1969, when Father Bergoglio was ordained priest, most of the novices who had entered with him had left the Society. In that year, Father Arrupe appointed as provincial Father Ricardo O'Farrell, under whom things took a marked turn for the worse. By 1973, the Province had lost close on half its numbers from ten years before and had only nine men in formation, against the hundred it had recently known. The Jesuit training was put into the hands of superiors who abandoned spirituality for sociology and Hegelian dialectics. The University of Salvador in Buenos Aires, which was under the Province's direction, fell into chaos; a number of priests teaching there left to marry their girl students, and the university ran up a debt of two million dollars. In this plight, a group of Jesuits petitioned Father Arrupe for O'Farrell's removal, and for once the general put survival before liberal idealism: Father Bergoglio was put in to pull the Province together. And this he did exceptionally well. In the six years he was provincial, he imposed order, and the Province began to recover. By the early 1980s there were some hundred students in the philosophical and theological seminary, even more than in the palmy days before the decline. Few Provinces in the Society in those troubled times could boast such a flourishing.

Central to Father Bergoglio's achievement was a rejection of the Marxist school that had taken over the Society in most of Latin America. There was a specific reason for this: Bergoglio himself was a man of the people, and in Latin America "liberation theology" was a movement of intellectuals from the higher classes, the counterpart of the radical chic that led the bourgeoisie in Europe to worship Sartre and Marcuse. With such attitudes Bergoglio had no sympathy; although he had not yet identified himself explicitly with the "theology of the people," which arose in direct competition with the Marxist school, his instinct made him follow the populist line of Peronism, which (whatever the cynicism of its creator) was more in touch with the genuine working class and lower middle class. Thus, Father Bergoglio backed the apostolate to the slum districts, but he did not want their inhabitants recruited as left-wing guerrillas, as some of his priests were trying to do. His way of dealing with the stricken Salvador University was indicative: he handed it over to some of his associates in the Peronist Guardia de Hierro, thus simultaneously ridding the Jesuit Province of its burden and presenting his political allies with a field of influence. A common accusation against Father Bergoglio was that he was a divisive figure as provincial. Given the state of the Province as he found it, with a party of highly political figures who had been dragging it to disaster, one might think that this was inevitable, or even a good thing; but the reports are that his methods were rather in the direction of exacting loyalty to himself and marginalizing those who failed to toe the line.

The six years during which Bergoglio was provincial were politically eventful ones in Argentina. His appointment in July 1973 coincided with Perón's return from his Spanish exile. Perón was triumphantly elected president that October and died in office the following July. He was succeeded as president by his widow Isabel, under whom the country slid into civil war, promoted by Cuban-backed guerrilla insurgents who formed, in Argentina, the largest such force in the Western Hemisphere. Isabel Perón unleashed death squads against them, which in turn paved the way to an open military takeover in March 1976, setting up a dictatorship that lasted for the next seven years. The repression was harsh, with many arrests, executions, and torture of political enemies.

As provincial, Father Bergoglio was responsible for several hundred Jesuits, many of whom had been radicalized in the previous decade, and many have questioned his relationship with the military dictatorship that was waging a so-called "dirty" war against Marxist subversion during this time. In 1986, author Emilio Mignone wrote a book alleging that Bergoglio had handed over two left-wing priests, Father Yorio and Father Jalics, to arrest and torture.[5] The accusation surfaced again in 2005, when Bergoglio was archbishop of Buenos Aires, and he had a biography of himself published to counter the charges.[6] Cardinal Bergoglio denied responsibility for the arrest of the two priests and stated that under the military regime he had helped a number of wanted men to escape the authorities. There were those who received these claims with skepticism, since nothing had been heard about them in the previous quarter-century. Father Jalics, who was by then the only survivor of the two Jesuits imprisoned, continued to blame the provincial for his betrayal, but he withdrew the accusation after Bergoglio was elected pope.

This is no place to explore the question of fact, but it may be worth quoting a cynical comment made by a bishop who knew Bergoglio well, as reported by Omar Bello: "Bergoglio would never have acted in such a direct and vulgar manner.... If you want to look at it more harshly, he would never have ruined his career with such a mistake."[7] One should remark that Father Bergoglio at that stage could hardly have been looking forward to a future as a bishop, let alone as pope; but following a Jesuit career to emulate the great Ledochówski might not have been absent from his thinking. Austen Ivereigh tells us that, after his harsh experience, Father Yorio viewed Bergoglio as devious, power-obsessed, and duplicitous. He was of course a biased judge, but (though one would not guess it from Ivereigh's respectful account) there were more impartial observers in Argentina who developed the same opinion.

Bishop and Archbishop

After six years as provincial, Father Bergoglio was made rector of the philosophical and theological seminary, which, as already mentioned, was by then full of students, and it doubled its numbers under his rule. But the radicals hated him, partly for his record as provincial and partly for his religious style, which was to stress the value of "popular" religion and to encourage devotions such as the veneration of images, which the Marxist intellectuals regarded with contempt. In 1986, a new Argentinian provincial was appointed who was a throwback to the O'Farrell regime of the early 1970s; vocations plummeted once more, and, as for Father Bergoglio, his days in authority were numbered. He was packed off to Germany, ostensibly to work for a doctorate on the Catholic philosopher Romano Guardini, but that was never completed. At the end of the year, Bergoglio returned to Argentina, without troubling to obtain permission, an act that was later to make the Jesuit general accuse him of disobedience. For a short time he taught theology in Buenos Aires, but he was a marked man with those in charge of the Argentinian Province; by 1990 he had been banished to an obscure post in a provincial town.

In worldly terms Father Bergoglio's career seemed over, and he spent two years dejected about his prospects; but the Society of Jesus and its left-wingers were not the entire Church. Bergoglio was rescued from his exile by the new archbishop of Buenos Aires, Cardinal Quarracino, who was a churchman of a different school. Like Bergoglio, Quarracino was a man of the people; and as a supporter of John Paul II's, he no doubt sympathized with that pope's action in 1981 when, in an unprecedented intervention, he deposed Father Arrupe as general of the Jesuits and tried to steer the Society into a less destructive course. The new general, elected in 1983, was Father Peter Kolvenbach, who in fact made little change of policy. In 1991, Cardinal Quarracino offered to make Father Bergoglio auxiliary bishop in Buenos Aires, and we should realize how exceptional this proposal was. Traditionally Jesuits are not allowed to accept episcopal appointments, and, except in missionary sees, a Jesuit bishop in the Latin American hierarchy was almost unheard of; but by such a promotion Bergoglio would be released from the Jesuit structure of command and enter one where his own populist theology was more accepted.

Since Father Bergoglio, as a Jesuit, would need a dispensation to be appointed, it was necessary to obtain a report from his order, for which Cardinal Quarracino applied in 1991. It was provided by the Jesuit general, and it represents the most damning character study of Jorge Bergoglio composed by anyone before his election as pope. The text of the report has never been made public, but the following account is given by a priest who had access to it before it disappeared from the Jesuit archive: Father Kolvenbach accused Bergoglio of a series of defects, ranging from habitual use of vulgar language to deviousness, disobedience concealed under a mask of humility, and lack of psychological balance; with a view to his suitability as a future bishop, the report pointed out that he had been a divisive figure as provincial of his own order. It is not surprising that, on being elected pope, Francis made efforts to get his hands on the existing copies of the document, and the original filed in the official Jesuit archives in Rome has disappeared. As regards the fairness of the report, we ought to allow for the hostility of the Jesuits who were in control in Argentina at the time, but in reality Bergoglio had exaggerated his order's hostility to him so as to pose as a martyr to Cardinal Quarracino (the phenomenon that Father Kolvenbach may have had in mind when he referred to disobedience under a mask of humility). When due allowance is made, the Kolvenbach Report can hardly be read as the depiction of a model religious by his superior.

Cardinal Quarracino, however, was determined to have Bergoglio as bishop and, although it took him a special audience with

Pope John Paul II, he got his way. In 1992, Father Bergoglio was duly appointed one of the several auxiliary bishops of Buenos Aires. In that office, he followed the line of his archbishop, who was regarded as being on the Right of the Church, in the populist style of John Paul II. The new hierarchical career which Quarracino's intervention had opened up for him was not long in blossoming. In 1997, Bishop Bergoglio was granted the right of succession, and the following year, on Cardinal Quarracino's death, he became archbishop of Buenos Aires; his appointment was at that time welcomed in conservative sectors. In February 2001, he received the cardinal's hat from Pope John Paul II.

Cardinal Bergoglio thus became Argentina's most prominent churchman, and there is no shortage of accounts of him as he was seen inside and outside the Church. Perhaps the most penetrating study of his personality was the one that was published by Omar Bello, *El Verdadero Francisco* (*The Real Francis*), within a few months of his election as pope. It is worth mentioning that this book vanished from the bookshops with unaccountable speed and is now unobtainable, a fate suffered by some other publications that were not favorable to Pope Francis. Omar Bello was a public relations executive who in 2005 was engaged to launch a new Church television channel which President Menem had gifted to the archdiocese of Buenos Aires, and over eight years he was to work for the archbishop and get to know him. As a professional in the field himself, Bello was quick to detect in Cardinal Bergoglio an accomplished self-promoter, disguised behind an image of simplicity and austerity. Bello moved in the circles of the archiepiscopal staff and got to hear the many stories that circulated about their enigmatic superior.

Probably the best known of these is the one of Félix Bottazzi, an employee whom the archbishop decided one day to dispense with, and he arranged his dismissal without showing his hand.[8] After he had been dismissed, Mr. Bottazzi sought an interview with Cardinal Bergoglio, who received him with friendly confusion: "But I knew nothing about it, my son. You surprise me.... What did they sack you for? Who did it?" Mr. Bottazzi did not get his job back, but Bergoglio presented him with a new car, and he went away convinced that the cardinal was a saint, pushed by forces beyond his control and dominated by a circle of malicious subordinates.

From Bello's description, this way of dealing with people may have been as much temperamental as political; he quotes the account of a priest who worked for Bergoglio and thought him his friend: "He manipulated me for years.... The guy manipulates you with the affections. You think he's your daddy and he strings you along."[9]

Also well-known is the story of a psychiatrist in Buenos Aires who specializes in treating members of the clergy. Among his patients were several priests on the archiepiscopal staff, who came to him exhausted from the merry dance they were being led by their superior. After listening to their troubles the psychiatrist said to one of them: "I can't treat you. To solve your problems I would need to treat your Archbishop."

Another writer who sheds light on the subject is Professor Lucrecia Rego de Planas, who knew Cardinal Bergoglio personally over a period of years; on September 23, 2013, she published a "Letter to Pope Francis."[10] She described with puzzlement Bergoglio's habit of being apparently on everybody's side in succession:

"one day chatting spiritedly with Mons. Duarte and Mons. Aguer [noted conservatives] about the defense of life and the Liturgy and, the same day, at supper, chatting just as spiritedly with Mons. Ysern and Mons. Rosa Chávez about base communities [the Soviet-style groups promoted by the "liberation theology" movement] and the terrible barriers represented by 'the dogmatic teachings' of the Church. One day a friend of Cardinal Cipriani Thorne [the Opus Dei archbishop of Lima] and Cardinal Rodríguez Maradiaga [of Honduras], talking about business ethics and against the ideologies of the New Age, and shortly afterwards a friend of Casaldáliga and Boff [the liberation theology celebrities], talking about class warfare."

The reason why Professor Rego de Planas was puzzled was that she was Mexican. If she had been Argentinian, she would have found the technique perfectly familiar: it has the note of classic Peronism. The story is told that Perón, in his days of glory, once proposed to induct a nephew in the mysteries of politics. He first brought the young man with him when he received a deputation of Communists; after hearing their views, he told them, "You're quite right." The next day he received a deputation of fascists and replied again to their arguments, "You're quite right." Then he asked his nephew what he thought and the young man said, "You've spoken with two groups with diametrically opposite opinions and you told them both that you agreed with them. This is completely unacceptable." Perón replied, "You're quite right too." An anecdote like this is an illustration of why no one can be expected to assess Pope Francis unless he understands the tradition of Argentinian politics, a phenomenon outside the rest of the world's experience; the Church has been taken by surprise by Francis because it has not had the key to him: he is Juan Perón in ecclesiastical translation. Those who seek to interpret him otherwise are missing the only relevant criterion.

For all this general complaisance, Omar Bello also speaks of those who were known as "'the widows of Bergoglio,' people who left their jobs, sat down in the chair that the cardinal brought them and at last were 'punished' for taking too much of a liberty." This can be related to another trait of Bergoglio's, his mistrust of people. To his collaborators he was, as one of them expressed it, "as suspicious as a one-eyed cow,"[11] above all in money matters. That is why he made a practice of surrounding himself with mediocrities whom he could dominate, a phenomenon seen both in his archiepiscopal staff in Buenos Aires and in the Argentinian hierarchy whose appointments he controlled. Bello adds: "I would be lying if I said that I don't know people who have a profound fear of him, and who move around his person with extreme caution. The situation became worse when he left for Rome, and stopped calling many of those who believed that they were his friends."

Bergoglio was not at ease with people who were in a position to overshadow him psychologically, intellectually, or socially. He was a recruit from a lower social level than many of his companions in the Society of Jesus, and in the class-conscious society that is Argentina's legacy from its oligarchic past this was always a visible handicap. He dealt with it by affecting an exaggerated vulgarity (thus leading to the complaints about coarse language mentioned in the Kolvenbach Report), while at large gatherings he would make a point of ignoring the bigwigs and spending time chatting genially to the cleaners and manual workers. One can see a similar defense mechanism in his assumption of a simple, retiring persona which was in fact a cover for close psychological control.

Bergoglio Moves to the Left

The political interest that had always marked Bergoglio became a dominant feature of his role as archbishop of Buenos Aires. During his time there, he faced the left-wing and anti-clerical government of Néstor Kirchner and his widow Cristina, who succeeded him as president in 2007. Bergoglio's strategy was to outflank the government on the Left: when the Kirchners attacked the Church with measures like the legalization of homosexual marriage, the cardinal riposted that the government was neglecting the real interests of the people. He cultivated influence with the Argentinian trade unions, and his rivalry with the government reached the point that Kirchner began to regard him as the real leader of the opposition. On this, we may read Austen Ivereigh's uncritical comment: "It was a very Bergoglio paradox. The austere, incorruptible mystic at war with spiritual worldliness—the pastoral bishop who smelled of sheep—was the most astutely political Argentine since Perón."[12] The political point can be accepted, but it begs the question to what extent the smell of sheep was an applied aroma, and how much the mysticism was part of the manifesto. By about 2010 Cardinal Bergoglio's political stance had exacerbated Church-State relations to such a point that some sectors in the Church were seeking to replace him as archbishop of Buenos Aires, proposing to have him compensated with a Roman appointment as prefect of the Congregation of Religious.[13]

Up to his arrival as archbishop of Buenos Aires in 1998, and even for a little time after it, Bergoglio was known to the public as the right-hand man of the "reactionary" Cardinal Quarracino, as the enemy of the Marxists in the Society of Jesus, even perhaps as a tacit collaborator with the military regime of the 1970s (although the sharpest criticisms on that score did not emerge until 2005). He was close to conservative groups in the Church such as Opus Dei and two Italian movements, Comunione e Liberazione and the Focolari, who were influential in Argentina. The great riddle that we need to approach is his transformation into the man whom the liberal section in the Church, and notably the St. Gallen Group, turned to as their figurehead. To many this change is the major enigma of Bergoglio's career.

Here too, however, we may be up against the blind spot that comes from failing to grasp the Peronist background. Perón as president had no hesitation in veering from the Right to the extreme Left as it suited his quest for power, and in the early twenty-first century the conditions were present in the Church to make such change of direction seem astute. Pope John Paul II was in decline; there was a wide assumption that the next pope would be a liberal. Whether Bergoglio thought that he himself, after his elevation to the cardinalate in 2001, could be a credible successor is a point too far for speculation—a pope from Latin America might still appear a long shot. But there would be no harm in being on the (supposedly) winning side.

Cardinal Bergoglio's emergence before an international audience came by an accident of history. In October 2001 he attended the Synod of Bishops in Rome, held to debate the subject of the role of bishops in the Church. Bergoglio was subordinate to

Cardinal Egan of New York, who was due to deliver the *relatio*, or summing-up, at the end of the week-long meeting. But Egan was called away to attend a memorial service for the victims of the September 11 terrorist attack a few weeks previously, and the task unexpectedly fell to Cardinal Bergoglio. His speech made a great impression on the bishops. Austen Ivereigh emphasizes its role in establishing Bergoglio's reputation: "What he produced was concise and elegant and won plaudits all round.... Inside the hall, Bergoglio received high praise for the way he reflected the bishops' concerns without causing disunity. 'What people admired him for was how he rescued the best of the synod debate despite the limitations of the structure and method,' recalls Bergoglio's long-standing friend in Rome, Professor Guzmán Carriquiry."[14] What has not been revealed is that Cardinal Bergoglio's speech was written for him, from beginning to end, by the Argentinian priest Monsignor Daniel Emilio Estivill, a member of the Synod's secretariat. Those who know Monsignor Estivill report that he has been living ever since in a state of nervous suspense, for fear of the reprisals to which his inconvenient secret might expose him.

The Synod of Bishops helped Cardinal Bergoglio to make himself known to many leaders of the Church, including Cardinal Martini, whom he had first met at the Jesuit General Congregation of 1973. Martini, the cardinal archbishop of Milan, was the most formidable representative of the liberal wing of the Church, with every prospect of becoming the next pope, apart from the disadvantage of his age. For Bergoglio it was a strategy that cost nothing to signal himself as the ally of that party. He benefited from the glamour liberals attributed to the Latin American Church for its "liberation theology," even though that theology was not Bergoglio's own.

As the liberals' candidate, and alternative to Cardinal Ratzinger, he came close to election in the Conclave of 2005, and he returned to Argentina with the prestige of being the Latin American "nearly pope." There was a feeling, indeed, that he had been cheated of the papacy by the revelations published earlier in 2005 of his alleged betrayal of priests to Argentina's military dictatorship. A dossier on the subject had been distributed to the cardinals. On this score, Omar Bello comments that Bergoglio was lucky in his accuser, Horacio Verbitsky, a bitter Marxist and anti-clerical, whose evidence was accordingly discounted. In reply, Bergoglio had a biography of himself published, in the form of a series of interviews, rebutting the charges and claiming to have worked against the dictatorship.

The years just after 2005 were those of Cardinal Bergoglio's highest influence in Argentina and in Latin America. He had by now positioned himself as the enemy of the Right wing in the Church and assumed a fully liberal stance, to the dismay of those who had looked to him as the champion of Catholic values. His method was to make declarations that would satisfy Rome of his orthodoxy, while avoiding any serious opposition to the Kirchners' anti-Catholic program in Argentina. In 2010, when legislation to introduce homosexual marriage was brought in, Cardinal Bergoglio wrote a letter to some nuns asserting Christian doctrine in robust terms, but at the same time he discountenanced any effective opposition that Catholic activists wished to present. In that year, the traditionalist Catholic writer Antonio Caponnetto published a book, *La Iglesia Traicionada* (*The Church*

Betrayed), decrying "the embarrassing Gandhi-style magisterium which today paralyses him and with which he confuses and makes cowards of the flock entrusted to him,"[15] in contrast to the open defense of Catholic principle for which Bergoglio had been known only a few years before.

Bergoglio's Vatican Links

His new posture made Bergoglio an object of suspicion to the papal nuncio in Argentina, Archbishop Bernardini, and to prelates including Héctor Aguer, who was archbishop of La Plata. Indeed, after six or seven years of sparring, the opposition he suffered from these sectors came to eclipse his own influence, and was to lead to a sharp settling of scores when he became pope. But even before that elevation Bergoglio was not short of means to fight back. One of them was the perennial influence of money in Curial politics, at a time when the Vatican was struggling with the embarrassments bequeathed to it by the mismanagement of the Vatican Bank by Archbishop Marcinkus. As archbishop of Buenos Aires, Cardinal Bergoglio was *ex officio* chancellor of the Pontifical Catholic University of Argentina, which had a rich endowment of $200 million. For no clear reason, a large part of this money was transferred to the Vatican Bank. The transaction recalls a scandal years previously when Bergoglio had been auxiliary bishop of Buenos Aires and the archdiocese repudiated a debt of ten million dollars, on the grounds that the check issued by the archiepiscopal Curia had not been correctly signed. Austen Ivereigh gives a whitewashing account of this incident,[16] presenting Bergoglio as the reformer who cleaned up the mess, but the truth is that, as Cardinal Quarracino's right-hand man at the time, he must have had inside knowledge of how the check was issued, and the facts were never satisfactorily explained. These cases are just two examples of obscurities which suggest that the whole question of financial dealings during Bergoglio's tenure in Buenos Aires would repay special study by a researcher expert in the genre.

Another means of influence for Cardinal Bergoglio was his personal contacts. In Rome he had a friend in Cardinal Giovanni Battista Re, who was prefect of the Congregation of Bishops from 2000 to 2010. Cardinal Re began as a devoted ally of Bergoglio's, but like so many of Bergoglio's associates eventually had second thoughts and turned against him. During the honeymoon period, Bergoglio took advantage of their friendship to plant in the Congregation of Bishops the Argentinian priest Fabián Pedacchio, who became his agent and informant. Father Pedacchio sent Cardinal Bergoglio a stream of information by telephone calls and faxes, advising him of the letters that were received in the Congregation for Bishops, even those under the seal of secrecy. Through this ally, Bergoglio had a number of followers appointed bishops not only in Argentina but in other South American hierarchies. On being elected pope, Bergoglio rewarded Father Pedacchio by making him his private secretary, an appointment from which he continues to exercise his former influence.

The most noteworthy case in which Bergoglio used Father Pedacchio was in his feud with the Opus Dei bishop Rogelio Livieres, who headed the diocese of Ciudad del Este. Although this city is in Paraguay, it is close to the Argentinian frontier, and Bishop Livieres was himself Argentinian by origin. He was a staunch traditionalist, and as such he represented a challenge not only to Bergoglio but to liberals throughout the South American hierarchy. In his own diocese Livieres had founded a seminary that offered traditional priestly formation and was by all measures a signal success. At its height, the Ciudad del Este seminary had 240 students, more than all the other Paraguayan dioceses combined. It also attracted refugees from Cardinal Bergoglio's own seminary in Buenos Aires, which was not in a happy state, and this did not help Bergoglio to look kindly on his rival. The most notorious member of the Paraguayan hierarchy was Fernando Lugo, bishop of San Pedro, who abandoned his ministry for a political career and became president of the country, until he was impeached by his parliament in 2012. Before that, he had been combining his episcopal life with a string of affairs and fathered a number of illegitimate children. Bishop Livieres was alone in denouncing both Bishop Lugo and his colleagues in the Paraguayan hierarchy who had conspired to keep Lugo's misconduct secret.

In 2008, shortly after Lugo's election as president, Bishop Livieres paid an *ad limina* visit to Pope Benedict XVI and personally handed him a letter, under seal, in which he criticized the system of appointments that had managed to produce Bishop Lugo. His precautions did not prevent the letter from being passed to Cardinal Bergoglio and thence leaked to the press, with the successful intention of damaging Bishop Livieres with the Paraguayan government and with the rest of his hierarchy.[17] This proved merely a foretaste of the treatment the bishop was to receive under Pope Francis, when he was dismissed from office within a year of the papal election and his seminary disbanded.

One lesson we may draw from these disagreements: it was nearly forty years since the young Father Bergoglio had been appointed provincial of the Argentinian Jesuits in a moment of crisis; times had changed, but the veteran cardinal archbishop, in conflict with the national government, with the papal nuncio to his country, with a large section within his own Church, and even with bishops across the frontier, had not lost his talent for being a divisive force.

The revelations about Father Pedacchio and Bishop Livieres were made by the Spanish journalist Francisco José de la Cigoña well before Bergoglio was elected pope. De la Cigoña identified another agent Cardinal Bergoglio had in Rome, the Argentinian priest Guillermo Karcher, who was in the Protocol department of the Secretariat of State. In Buenos Aires, Bergoglio's auxiliary bishop, Eduardo García, had the job of managing "opinion" on bishops and other clergy on the internet. After describing this system of control, de la Cigoña commented: "That is how Bergoglio proceeds to generate a network of lies, intrigue, espionage, mistrust and, more effective than anything, fear. It is the opinion of an Argentinian official who works in the Vatican and who, out of fear of course, prefers not to be named: Bergoglio 'is a person who above all else knows how to instil fear.' That is why he has an influence in the Holy See which surprises many. However much he may work carefully to impress everyone with the appearance of a plaster saint, austere and mortified, he is a man with a mentality of power. And he always was."[18] In reporting these perceptions to a Spanish readership, de la Cigoña was passing on the estimate which many in Argentina had by then formed of their archbishop, but which unfortunately had not reached the knowledge of the world's cardinals when they met for the Conclave of 2013.

The position that Bergoglio built up in these years was threatened, however, by a looming deadline. In December 2011, on reaching the age of seventy-five, he would have to submit his resignation as archbishop, and churchmen in Argentina began to abandon him. Omar Bello considers that by 2011 Bergoglio had been eclipsed in influence by his rival Héctor Aguer, archbishop of La Plata. Pope Benedict in fact refused Bergoglio's resignation (to the disgust of some members of the Argentinian hierarchy, who would soon suffer for their discontent) and asked the retiring prelate to continue for a little longer. But Cardinal Bergoglio felt and looked like a lame duck; he openly talked about withdrawing to a retirement home for the clergy. The hopes that had been raised in the 2005 Conclave had all but disappeared.

A Pope Abdicates

Unexpectedly, however, this gloomy situation was transformed by a rumor from Rome. By the middle of 2012, a few insiders in the Curia knew that Pope Benedict was considering abdication; he had confided his intention to two of his closest associates, the secretary of state Cardinal Bertone, and the papal secretary Archbishop Gänswein, and he had named the exact date: February 28, 2013. Cardinal Bergoglio's communications with Rome were abruptly stepped up, rising to hectic levels as the date of Pope Benedict's rumored abdication approached.[19] Sure enough, on February 11, 2013, Pope Benedict made his public announcement to the cardinals, and it took almost the whole world by surprise; not Bergoglio and his associates, however, as eyewitnesses discovered. On the day of the announcement itself, the rector of Buenos Aires cathedral went to visit his cardinal and found him exultant. During their interview, the telephone never stopped ringing with international calls from Bergoglio's allies, and they were all calls of personal congratulations. One Argentinian friend, however, less well informed than the others, rang up to ask about the extraordinary news, and Bergoglio told him: "You don't know what this means."[20]

Cardinal Bergoglio had had eight years to mull exactly what it meant. In 2005, the plans of the St. Gallen Group had seemed shattered by the election of Benedict XVI. It was assumed that Benedict was due for a reign of ten or even fifteen years, and that would be too long for any of those involved to benefit. The abdication in February 2013 came just in time to revive the St. Gallen program. Cardinal Martini had died the previous year, but Danneels and Kasper were just young enough to beat the exclusion from papal conclaves that cardinals incur at the age of eighty, a milestone they would both reach later in the year. Above all, Bergoglio, at the age of seventy-six, remained *papabile*; the extension of his mandate by Pope Benedict meant that he was still in place as archbishop of Buenos Aires, and thus a leading member of the Latin American hierarchy.

Over the next two weeks, before he traveled to Rome for Pope Benedict's official farewell, Bergoglio was in a fever of activity, cloaked in an appearance of indifference. A priest who knew him confided to Omar Bello that the cardinal was making a circus of not wanting to go to Rome, "and I knew that he was talking to half the world and plotting like mad. Well, that's Jorge...."[21] Yet anyone who imagined him circularizing the College of Cardinals with "Vote for me" messages would have underestimated Jorge. His strategy from the first was to present himself as a supporter of Cardinal Seán O'Malley of Boston. Omar Bello explains the ploy as follows: it would distract the attention of the European cardinals from his own bid, yet Bergoglio knew that for the Latin Americans, and indeed for many others in the Church, a pope from the United States was anathema; it savored too much of Yankee imperialism. But to press for O'Malley was *ipso facto* to direct attention to the American continent; if the cardinals rejected O'Malley they might turn to Bergoglio, as his Latin American counterpart. This is a possible interpretation, though it seems over-tortuous. As an alternative, one could point to the disclosure by Cardinal McCarrick of Washington that an Italian layman visited him just before the Conclave to urge him to "talk up" Bergoglio.[22] On this reading, by canvassing for O'Malley, Bergoglio was simply signalling to the North American cardinals that he was their ally.

What few people would dispute is that the Conclave of 2013 was probably the most political papal election since the fall of the Papal States. It would have been so merely for the dramatic background against which it was held, the abdication of a pope, the first time such a thing had happened for six hundred years. But even more pressing were the circumstances that had led to it: the running sore of the Vatican finances, which had defied efforts to solve it for years; the "Vatileaks" scandal of 2012, when the pope's butler had revealed secret papers precisely to show how impotent Benedict XVI was to control the disorder around him; and finally the private report that was circulated in December 2012, revealing such moral corruption in the Curia that it was thought to be the last straw in persuading Benedict that he could no longer cope. One thing was obvious: the job of the next pope would be to clear up a morass. It is therefore more pertinent to say that the Conclave of 2013 was the most panicky papal election for centuries. People were looking for a savior, and that is not necessarily the frame of mind in which to make a good choice.

It is generally thought that Pope Benedict's purpose in abdicating was to bring about the succession of Cardinal Scola, archbishop of Milan, and he charged the secretary of state Bertone with managing the Conclave accordingly. Scola was doctrinally in the same line as Benedict, and he seemed the strong man capable of dealing with the troubles heaping themselves on the Holy See. What Benedict did not realize was that there was little chance of the other Italian cardinals agreeing to vote for Scola, whom they regarded as a careerist. What was worse, Bertone himself did not want Scola, and his response to the papal commission was simply to ignore it. The Benedict plan thus failed from the start, and the Conclave was thrown wide open. With no other lead, the machine reset itself to 2005, and the St. Gallen Group came to life again, after its eight-year entombment.

The St. Gallen cardinals were mainly influential with the Europeans, but they had some contacts beyond them. Murphy-O'Connor was busy among the English-speaking cardinals from Africa and Asia, and other Africans were brought over by

Cardinal Monsengwo, a protégé of Danneels. Austen Ivereigh repeats the story of Murphy-O'Connor warning Bergoglio to "be careful" because it was his turn now, to which the reply was *capisco*; but this was like a three-year-old giving parenting advice to his mother. The liberal cardinals thought that they were using Bergoglio; it is more likely that he was using them. There was no reason to think that the St. Gallen Group was any more capable of delivering a majority in the Conclave in 2013 than it had been in 2005. The crucial constituency were the North American cardinals, and Bergoglio had already taken care of them himself. The Latin Americans would vote for him too, encouraged by the near miss of 2005.

Ivereigh's account gives a good idea of the intense politicking that went on at the 2013 Conclave. Bergoglio's supporters, instructed by their experience eight years before, concentrated on making sure that their man got at least twenty-five votes in the first scrutiny, a result essential to give him momentum. This was achieved, and on the second day, March 13, Bergoglio was comfortably ahead in the second ballot of the morning, with fifty votes. That afternoon, the fourth vote produced a hitch: a blank voting-paper was accidentally included among the papers counted, and that invalidated the scrutiny. The rules for papal conclaves lay down that only four scrutinies should take place on any day, but curiously this was ignored, and a fifth vote was held as if the fourth had not taken place. In this, Bergoglio was elected with more than ninety-five votes out of the 115 cast. Catholic journalist Antonio Socci has contended forcefully that this fifth ballot of the day was null and void,[23] but canon lawyers have disputed the point, considering it debatable. Whether one chooses to uphold Socci's view or not, it seems appropriate that the political heir of Juan Perón should have been raised to the head of the Catholic Church by what was arguably an invalid vote.

Chapter 3

REFORM? WHAT REFORM?

From the moment Jorge Bergoglio was elected pope, he made it clear that he was going to be different. Observers who had dealt with him before already knew what to expect. Professor Lucrecia Rego de Planas noted how she would attend meetings with bishops and they would drive up, on time, in their cars, whereas Bergoglio would arrive late, in a flurry, loudly explaining his vicissitudes on public transport. Her reaction was "Phew! What an itch to attract attention!" and she found that many others had the same impression.[1] Thus also, when Francis became pope, he would not use the traditional papal pectoral cross, or the ring, or the shoes, or the chair, but had others of less splendor. Famously, he refused to move into the old papal apartment overlooking St. Peter's Square and had rooms set aside for himself in the Casa Santa Marta, the guesthouse for visiting cardinals, where he has lived ever since. One of his most self-effacing gestures happened the morning after his election; he went to the guesthouse where he had been staying during the Conclave to pay his bill in person. In keeping with the humility of the occasion, the television cameras were there to film him. On the same day, he telephoned his barber at home, and his dentist, to cancel an appointment, and his news agent, to cancel his newspapers, and made sure the press knew about it.

The media all lapped it up, as they had in Buenos Aires when he traveled by the city underground (with his press secretary present, and a photographer to record it). There was no doubt that here was a pope who outdid all others in humility. Other popes, over the past hundred years, came from backgrounds at least as lowly as Jorge Bergoglio's (including the "Peasant Popes" Pius X and John XXIII), but on being elected to the papal throne they had accepted the traditional symbols of their office. Bergoglio distinguished himself to an international audience not only by his gestures of humility but by a newfound bonhomie that won all hearts. In Buenos Aires, one Argentinian Catholic had nicknamed Bergoglio *carucha* (grumpy-face) for his habitual demeanor as archbishop, but now his compatriots saw him turn into what Omar Bello called a papal Lassie, a figure whom they hardly recognized.

Professor Rego de Planas interpreted Cardinal Bergoglio's populist gestures when he was archbishop of Buenos Aires as part of an ingrained desire to be liked by everyone and to gain easy popularity; but after five years of Francis's pontificate we have to recognize that her diagnosis was too naïve. She had not fathomed what an accomplished politician Bergoglio is. He knows that in the modern world image is everything, and that a pope who has the secular media on his side can do things that other popes had not dreamt of; and that indeed was precisely his program. To the media, Francis was the great reformer elected to carry out a miraculous rejuvenation of the Church. No one troubled to notice that little sign of such rejuvenation appeared during his time as archbishop of Buenos Aires. During his fifteen years in office, the Catholic Church in Argentina suffered a 10 percent drop in membership; and the decline in members of the priesthood and the religious life was even worse. After five years as pope, there is no indication that Francis has rejuvenated the Catholic Church in any way. In real terms, the "Francis Effect" has proved a phenomenon confined to the media.

When the cardinals elected him, Pope Francis faced three major problems. One of them was the scandal of moral and political corruption in the Roman Curia, of which fresh evidence had been circulated in December 2012; another was that of sexual abuse among the clergy, a worldwide scandal that had been gathering pace for twenty years and which, by the time of Benedict XVI's pontificate, bid fair to destroy the Church's whole moral authority; and a third was also of long standing, the morass of the Vatican finances which had become a public scandal in John Paul II's reign and had so far resisted all attempts to tackle it.

What Happened to Reform of the Curia?

The Roman Curia is the central government of the Catholic Church. It is a large organization, including nine Congregations, twelve Pontifical Councils, six Pontifical Commissions, and three Tribunals. As one would expect of such a body, the question of its reform is not new. In considering its history, we may leave aside the period when the Curia had to administer the Papal States as well as the Church. After the fall of the Temporal Power in 1870, the Curia developed into an institution which, on the whole, was honest and efficient, and not unworthy of its function as the directing organism of the universal Church. It had the natural weaknesses of any bureaucracy, added to the local defects that it was overwhelmingly Italian in personnel and inclined to a traditional nepotism, especially in the little, non-clerical posts such as those of doorman or chauffeur.

If one had to point to a time when an undue material bias began to appear, it was perhaps the later years of Pius XII's reign, when that very able pope began to lose his personal control of affairs. By 1953, it was felt by many that the Curia had slipped into the hands of a clique of five cardinals, who were known disrespectfully as the Pentagon. Their leader was Nicola Canali, the Vatican's financial minister, who was famous for his close alliance with the papal bankers of the time and with the pope's nephew, the influential Prince Carlo Pacelli.

For all his reputation as a reformer, the problem was not tackled by the next pope, John XXIII, in his brief five years. Paul VI, who had spent almost his entire clerical career in Rome, came to the throne in 1963 with a laudable desire to reform the Curia, but his achievements fell short of his intentions. One thing he did succeed in doing was to internationalize its personnel, but this went along with a big jump in numbers, from 1,322 to 3,150, with all the implications of an overgrown bureaucracy.[2] Worse was Pope Paul's decision to put the entire Curia under the overall authority of the Secretariat of State. This was no doubt intended to introduce a measure of coordination, but it also meant that the vast majority of departments, whose function was purely religious, were subjected to the Vatican's political arm. And the worst mistake of all was what Pope Paul did with the Church's finances. These were put under the direction of Archbishop Paul Marcinkus, a no-frills cleric from Chicago who was unfortunately out of his depth in the world of international finance into which his appointment pitched him. His pragmatic approach to keeping the Vatican afloat economically led him into association with the Mafia bankers Michele Sindona and Roberto Calvi, with dire consequences when these were exposed. In 1987, a warrant was issued for Marcinkus's arrest, but Pope John Paul II, in an extraordinary preference for the Church's worldly prerogatives over its moral duty, chose to shelter him under the Vatican's sovereignty. The lessons were not learned under Marcinkus's successor, Bishop Donato de Bonis, who was dismissed in 1993 after further scandals and was incongruously appointed prelate (chief chaplain) of the Order of Malta, likewise to benefit from that body's extraterritorial privilege. Holed up for years in the Order's Roman headquarters, he did not dare step into the street for fear of arrest by the Italian police.

John Paul II had been elected in 1978 as a young, vigorous pope who was expected to deal with the Church's problems, but internal government was not his forte. From the beginning he devoted himself to high-profile globe-trotting visits, and he neglected the day-to-day demands of the organization that served him. His appointment of Cardinal Angelo Sodano as secretary of state in 1991 worsened an already decaying situation. The cronyism and corruption that Cardinal Sodano's regime aggravated included among its scandals the covering up of the sexual immoralities of the founder of the Legionaries of Christ, Father Marcial Maciel, because of the large sums that that powerful organization was able to contribute to the Vatican. With Cardinal Tarcisio Bertone, secretary of state from 2006 to 2013, the rot went in a different direction. Pope Benedict XVI, who appointed him, distanced himself from Curial affairs. Though Benedict had served in the heart of the Curia for twenty-four years before his election, his interests were academic rather than managerial or political, and he became a virtual hermit, with the result that the Curia, which needed papal leadership, descended into factional chaos.[3] In these conditions Cardinal Bertone had a free hand to pursue his own interests; he vastly enhanced the already overblown power of the Secretariat of State by planting his nominees in key places in every Congregation, Council, or Commission, and these were the men in charge when Pope Francis was elected. They formed a massive vested interest whose capacity to block the wishes of the pope himself had been one of the factors in persuading Benedict XVI to abdicate, convinced that he could no longer cope.

This situation had been brought dramatically into the public eye by the "Vatileaks" scandal of 2012. The affair was precipitated by the pope's butler, Paolo Gabriele, who decided to expose to the press the corruption that he saw around him. He simply picked up sensitive documents that were left in his shared office and handed them to journalist Gianluigi Nuzzi. Among the documents were letters exchanged between Monsignor Carlo Maria Viganò, Cardinal Bertone, and the pope himself. They revealed that Monsignor Viganò believed that he had been dismissed as secretary of the governorate because of his inconvenient zeal for reform. The leaks were made public on Italian television in the program *Gli intoccabili* in January 2012, and Nuzzi followed it up in May with his book *Sua Santità: Le carte segrete di Benedetto XVI*. The butler was tried in the Vatican's court and sentenced to eighteen months' imprisonment, but Benedict XVI pardoned him on December 22, 2012, recognizing that Gabriele had acted to expose an inexcusable network of manipulation and intrigue.

The timing of the pardon was not coincidental. Five days earlier Pope Benedict had received a secret report, prepared for him by Cardinals Herranz, De Giorgi, and Tomko, whom he had commissioned in March to investigate the leaks. The remit of the cardinals was to question dozens of witnesses and to study the situation in the Vatican which the leaked documents revealed, and what they found was horrendous. They showed a picture not only of a Vatican machine that was going its own way regardless of the wishes of the pope, but also of a moral corruption that had long been known to insiders but to which nobody had hitherto put names. The report itself has never been made public, but the substance of its accusations was disclosed in various asides and revelations over the next few years. Details emerged of a homosexual network within the Vatican which was in collusion to promote its own interests. Prelates were employing laymen with criminal records who cruised the Roman bars and night clubs to procure boys for them, and they were rewarded with protected careers in the Vatican. One monsignor was tailed on visits to homosexual massage parlors and was blackmailed with photographs of the encounters. Stories went around of prelates who were known by female names, in broad hints at their proclivities, and of secretaries who were being paid 15,000 euros a month, for services obviously not confined to the office.[4]

Pope Francis was elected with the expectation that he would reform the Curia, beginning with the Secretariat of State, which had grown far too powerful and was the chief reason the Curia had become so corrupted with secular influence.

One month after his election, Pope Francis appointed a council of eight cardinals to oversee the process of reform. Another cardinal was added later and they are now known as the C9. Up to June 2017 there were eighteen meetings of this council, which have resulted in only token reforms, such as merging a few Pontifical Councils. Overall, the effect has been nil. The secretary of one dicastery has commented: "Francis has made a lot of heads roll, perhaps too many, but the results are scarce. There are working commissions, there are study groups, there are consultancies, but nobody knows when anything concrete will be seen, or if it will ever be seen."[5]

Regarding the papal finances, the same official says: "It was Ratzinger who was the pope of the turn-around, Francis has slipped into that furrow, but in a rather muddled way.... The council of nine cardinals, the so-called C9, appointed by him to carry out the reform plans, has held many meetings without coming to any significant decisions. And then there is the question of synodal government. The Synod of Bishops, Francis has said, is being re-conceived, on the model of the Second Vatican Council, but in practice nobody knows how."[6]

The key to this failure may be found in a remark of Pope Francis himself: "I cannot carry out the reforms myself because I am very disorganized."[7] This is a euphemistic way of expressing the fact that Bergoglio's penchant has always been for disruption rather than construction. His famous slogan for the faithful was, *"Hagan lío"*—create a mess. This may (or may not) be a fruitful exhortation to zealous souls to break out of sloth and complacency, but it is not a very good principle for governing the Church, and even less is it a blueprint for administrative reform of an organization whose trouble was precisely that it was already an unholy mess before Francis arrived.

Pope Francis thus delegated the process of reform to the C9, but here too is a problem. These nine cardinals are an extremely disparate group; they are not distinguished by great personal records as administrators, and for the most part they have little experience of the Curia. They therefore bring to their work a somewhat superficial knowledge of the complex body they have to reform. If they were under a pope who showed strong administrative ability, they might be praised as bringing a fresh outside view; but under a pope who is likewise an outsider to the Curia they show all the weaknesses of a committee without clear leadership. Above all, their work is hamstrung by a pope who is more interested in playing power games than in overseeing reform. One aspect of this is that many of Pope Francis's changes have been driven by ideology rather than efficiency (for example, no one could say that the removal of Cardinal Burke as prefect of the Apostolic Signatura was justified by any considerations of integrity or competence), but the phenomenon goes a good deal deeper, as we will see.

The biggest question mark over the C9 emerged in December 2017, when accusations were made public about Cardinal Rodríguez Maradiaga's stewardship as archbishop of Tegucigalpa. The cardinal had been for many years Bergoglio's closest friend in the Latin American hierarchy, was a key figure in gathering support for him in the 2013 Conclave,[8] and has benefited correspondingly. In his capacity as president of the C9, he has been referred to by some as the "vice-pope." He has certainly been one of the chief spokesmen of Francis's pontificate and a leading advocate of "the Church of the poor." In May 2017, accusations were made regarding the misuse of more than $1.2 million that the cardinal was responsible for, together with the revelation of payment to him of some $600,000 by the University of Tegucigalpa.[9] The consequence of this was the dispatch of an apostolic envoy to Honduras, Bishop Casaretto, and it is now beginning to seem that the financial abuses are only the tip of the iceberg. The response of Pope Francis to his envoy's report has been, typically, to reserve the case to himself instead of allowing normal procedures to operate, but evidence is emerging of a level of corruption in the archdiocese of Tegucigalpa perhaps without parallel in the Catholic world. Cardinal Rodríguez Maradiaga is known to be particularly close to a bishop who has been accused of supporting a male companion out of diocesan funds, and during his visit Bishop Casaretto discovered allegations of sexual abuse, which have not been acted upon. At the time of writing, the scandal remains subject to a cover-up in which Pope Francis seems to be fully complicit.

These recent revelations, to put it mildly, call into question Cardinal Rodríguez Maradiaga's credentials as the leader of a movement to reform the Church, whether in financial, administrative, or moral matters, and the doubts are not laid to rest by his record hitherto as president of the C9. One result of the lack of good administrative judgment is that the proposed reforms in the Curia have staggered between inertia on the one hand and an ill-thought-out radicalism on the other. In the early months of Francis's pontificate there was a proposal to reduce the power of the Secretariat of State and rename its head the papal secretary, which is a completely different office.[10] In the event, nothing substantive was done. More recently, Cardinal Rodríguez Maradiaga has proposed fusing the Vatican's three tribunals—the Penitentiary, the Rota, and the Segnatura—into a single Dicastery of Justice. But one of the functions of the Segnatura is to hear appeals from the Rota. So either the reforming cardinals are ignorant of how the tribunals function or they do not care about creating a tribunal system from which there is no appeal (and both could be true).

The muddle and inefficiency that have characterized Francis's "reform" movement were highlighted in the American magazine *First Things* in June 2017.[11] The article by Marco Tosatti ("Waiting for Vatican Reform") noted that in September 2016 the Council for the Laity, Family, and Life, formally ceased to exist and was merged into a new dicastery under Cardinal Kevin Farrell. It took nearly a year for the Council's secretary to be named, in June 2017, and even then he was not expected to come to Rome for several months (he lived in Brazil), and his under-secretary had yet to be named. Without these key appointments in place, the dicastery was unable to do its work, and the staff of the old Council were still there, waiting to be dismissed, in what one of them described as an atmosphere of "placid, quiet chaos."

In August 2016, the new Dicastery for Promoting Integral Human Development was set up, with effect from January 1,

2017, and with the African Cardinal Peter Turkson as its prefect. The dicastery is supposed to be a merger of the Pontifical Councils for Justice and Peace, for Pastoral Care of Migrants and Itinerant People, and for Pastoral Assistance to Health Care Workers, together with *Cor Unum*. But Cardinal Turkson (who is a biblical scholar with no administrative experience) said in June 2017 that it was unclear to him what the dicastery was supposed to do, and he was still waiting for his marching orders. As of 2018, the vacancies in Cardinal Farrell's dicastery have been filled, but Cardinal Turkson does not seem closer to being on top of his responsibilities.

Summarizing the scant and superficial results of what the C9 has achieved, Tosatti quoted the comment of a cardinal and an archbishop who have worked in the Curia for many years: "Such a reform! We could have prepared it ourselves, in the space of one morning, sitting at a table."

A further step in the wrong direction is the result of Pope Francis's offhand ways. In the past there was a system which provided for each head of a Vatican body to see the pope regularly, usually twice a month; it was called the *udienza di tabella*. This has now been abolished; officials have to make special appointments, and they are often told that the pope is too busy. In the shadowy and controversial case of the pope's dismissal of three priests from the Congregation for the Doctrine of the Faith (on October 28, 2016), Cardinal Gerhard Müller asked many times for an audience to plead for the priests, whom he held in high esteem, only to be told to execute the order as given and without explanation.

The Secretariat of State has become a gatekeeper through whom all business has to pass, and a filter between the pope and the Curia. The secretariat has thus become more powerful than ever. While this arrangement lasts, reform is unlikely.

Journalists have propagated a misconception that Francis is a liberal pope battling against a phalanx of conservative clerics whose aim is to preserve papal power and oppose liberal reforms. The Curia was once conservative, but it has not been that way for decades, certainly since Pope Paul VI brought in as secretary of state a French prelate from outside the Curia, Jean-Marie Villot (1969–1979) who re-established the Curia on what might be called a French bureaucratic model. The old system, whatever its defects, was based on the moral principle of serving a traditional papal monarchy. The Villot system replaced that with bureaucrats who look after their own departments, in their own self-interest, and that has continued under the "liberal" Pope Francis. The faults that have been described so far are relative trivia, and at worst they would only illustrate Francis's lack of competence as a reformer. But the reality is in fact far blacker. It includes the state of chaotic rivalry and conflict which has been produced by Pope Francis's manipulative methods, and which will be described below as it affects the Secretariat of State, the Secretariat for the Economy, and the various Vatican financial bodies. And it extends to the moral state of the Curia, of which such a daunting picture was presented to Benedict XVI two months before his abdication. Any idea that Pope Francis has applied himself to reforming that aspect would be seriously astray. The existence of a homosexual lobby in the Vatican, which was revealed by the cardinals' report of December 2012, is a scandal which Pope Francis has taken no steps to correct, and which he has indeed accentuated. One of the most notorious cases is that of Monsignor

Battista Ricca, who is prelate of the Istituto delle Opere di Reli-gione. Monsignor Ricca made his career as a member of the papal diplomatic service. After a posting in Bern, he was sent to Uru-guay in 1999 and thoughtfully brought with him his boyfriend, Patrick Haari, a louche captain in the Swiss Army. Taking advan-tage of an interval between the retirement of the nuncio and the arrival of his successor, Ricca, as chargé d'affaires, settled Haari in the nunciature itself, with a job, a salary, and lodging. The new nuncio, arriving in Montevideo in early 2000, tried to get both Ricca and Haari out, but the former was protected by his friend-ship with Archbishop (later Cardinal) Re, who was at that time *sostituto* in the Secretariat of State. The ménage was an open scandal to the clergy and to the nuns who attended the Montevi-deo nunciature, but nothing could be done, even after Haari was brought home from a house of homosexual encounters where he had been beaten up by some rough trade. Not until Monsignor Ricca himself was caught in an illegal and compromising situation by the police, in August 2001, was the long-suffering nuncio able to get rid of his subordinate. After a further posting to Trinidad and Tobago, where he again quarreled with the nuncio, Ricca was finally removed from the active diplomatic service in 2005, when he was given a job in Rome with the status of councilor of a first-rank nunciature. His responsibilities included the management of the cardinals' guest-house in Via della Scrofa where Cardinal Bergoglio was wont to stay, and where he famously went to pay his bill on the morning after his election. Given that Montevideo faces Buenos Aires across the mouth of the River Plate, it seems unlikely that the then cardinal archbishop was unaware of the goings-on in the nunciature over the water, but that did not prevent him from striking up a close friendship with Monsignor Ricca, which stood the latter in good stead when Bergoglio was elected pope. Within three months of that event, in June 2013, Monsignor Ricca was appointed prelate of the Vatican Bank.[12] The appointment was the subject of a journalist's question to the pope a few weeks later, in one of his signature press conferences on board an aeroplane, when he was quizzed about this promotion of a notorious homosexual, and it drew from the pope the well-known comment, "Who am I to judge?" In fact, his patronage of Monsignor Ricca fits the pattern which was well established when he was archbishop of Buenos Aires, whereby he surrounds himself with morally weak people so as to have them under his thumb.

One may say that the average pious Catholic would be scandalized to know that the higher reaches of the Church are occupied by men who violate so blatantly their obligations of chastity as Monsignor Ricca has done, and would find it incredible that they are not only tolerated but protected and promoted. Yet that situation has not only continued unchecked under Pope Francis; it has visibly worsened. In October 2015, an official of the Congregation for the Doctrine of the Faith, Monsignor Krzysztof Charamsa, ostentatiously resigned his position, announced that he was an active homosexual, and launched, for the benefit of the press, a tirade against the Church's moral teaching. He also "revealed" the existence of a homosexual lobby in the Curia, which was indeed well known but thus received confirmation from the inside. The significant facts about this case were that Monsignor Charamsa had been working for years as a bitter opponent of the Church's teaching of which he was ostensibly a spokesman, and also that, with all the talk of cleaning up the Curia, no attempt has ever been made to disturb such figures; it took a gesture of defiance on his part to remove him from the office he had so plainly betrayed.

In June 2017 Monsignor Luigi Capozzi, the secretary of Cardinal Coccopalmerio, was caught by the Vatican's Gendarmeria hosting a homosexual drugs party in his luxurious apartment in the Palazzo del Sant'Uffizio. He had been using his car with Vatican number-plates in order to transport drugs without being stopped by the Italian police.[13] Cardinal Coccopalmerio, who is one of Pope Francis's foremost yes-men, had proposed this trusted assistant for a bishopric.

Pope Francis's liberalism has only given more power to the homosexual lobby in the Curia. He supported, for example, Archbishop Bruno Forte's attempt to insert a relaxation of Catholic teaching on homosexuality into the report of the 2014 Synod of the Family (his insertion was rejected). Perhaps an even more scandalous case is that of the notorious liberal (especially on matters regarding homosexuality) Archbishop Vincenzo Paglia, who, incredibly, is president of the Pontifical Council for the Family and whom Pope Francis has recently made president of the John Paul II Institute for Studies on Marriage and the Family, the body which John Paul intended as the watchdog of the Church's teaching. One of Archbishop Paglia's claims to fame is his commissioning of a prominent Argentinian homosexual artist to create a mural in his cathedral church that has been described as "homoerotic" and includes the archbishop himself in a net of nude or semi-nude bodies.[14]

In December 2014, Pope Francis took advantage of the Curia's gathering for Christmas greetings to harangue them, in inventive detail, on the fifteen ways in which they were corrupt. This approach to Curial reform illustrated Francis's taste for incessant naggings and recherché insults that distinguished him in his first years (he seems to have realized now that people are tired of it); but it also falls into a familiar pattern of rhetoric designed to show him as a radical reformer, but with no practical measures to follow. The true corruption in the Roman Curia, whether administrative or moral, is not something that Francis has so far shown any signs of reforming; on the contrary, it is a weakness that he has been exploiting and that has been growing under his government.

What Happened to "Zero Tolerance" for Clerical Sexual Offenders?

The phenomenon of widespread homosexuality among clergy and bishops had been public knowledge since at least 2001, when the *Boston Globe* began a series of exposés on the clergy sex abuse scandals. The John Jay Report, an investigation commissioned by the U.S. Conference of Catholic Bishops, published in 2004, found that more than 80 percent of the victims of clergy sexual abuse had been adolescent males.[15] Reports from dioceses around the world—including national bishops' conferences in Australia, Canada, Argentina, Brazil, Chile, Mexico, the Philippines, India, and most of Europe—found similar results.

The John Jay Report covered the period from 1950 to 2002 and found the complaints had peaked at a period coinciding with the vogue for ignoring or re-writing seminary admission guidelines to allow homosexuals to study and be ordained as priests—the 1960s to the 1980s—a period that can be likened to the Catholic Church's own internal Sexual Revolution. The Vatican itself was not immune to this global wave of sexual permissiveness. The broad parameters of the problem became clear in 2012 with the "Vatileaks" scandal that revealed an extensive and well-funded homosexual network operating out of the Curia, with Curial officials approving the use of Vatican-owned properties in Rome as homosexual brothels aimed at priestly clientele.

Despite attempts by the secular press to pin the blame retro-actively on Pope Benedict, the records show that the former head of the Congregation for the Doctrine of the Faith had undertaken significant and effective reforms, described in the United States as a "zero tolerance policy." Sexual abuse of minors, at least in 2001, was still a subject capable of arousing outrage among the public, and the demands for reform were loud. But even then, the homosexual lobby had made enormous strides in image manage-ment. The secular media collaborated, pinning the blame on sinister and creepy "clergy paedophiles," as distinguished from fresh-scrubbed and morally acceptable homosexual priests, while ignoring that the homosexual lobby favored lowering the legal age of consent to fourteen, the age preferred by homosexual clergy abusers.[16] These larger cultural shifts, and the reality inside the Vatican, perhaps explain why Pope Benedict's reforms—which included a ban on men with homosexual tendencies from the priesthood[17]—have availed so little, even before they were subverted by his successor.

According to data presented by the Congregation for the Doctrine of the Faith to the UN Human Rights Commission in January 2014, Benedict XVI had defrocked or suspended more than eight hundred priests for past sexual abuse between 2009 and 2012. These included the notorious Fr. Marcial Maciel, the influential founder of the Legionaries of Christ who under the previous pope had enjoyed immunity from investigation. In 2011, the Congregation for the Doctrine of the Faith sent a letter to the world's bishops' conferences, asking them to adopt stringent guidelines on how to respond to allegations of sexual abuse. The guidelines required bishops to make every effort to protect minors, assist victims, collaborate with civil authorities, and forward all new cases to the Congregation for the Doctrine of the Faith so that it could take action. In a March 2010 pastoral letter to Ireland's Catholics, Benedict criticized the lax application of the Church's laws and said the bishops' failures had "seriously undermined" their "credibility and effectiveness." He noted a "misguided tendency" against applying canonical punishments that he said was due to "misinterpretations of the Second Vatican Council."

The guidelines were merely reiterations of previous reforms Ratzinger had insisted upon as head of the Congregation for the Doctrine of the Faith. In April 2001, Pope John Paul II had issued norms[18] that required bishops to report all accusations of clerical "delicta graviora" (graver offences) against the Sixth Commandment to the Congregation for the Doctrine of the Faith, a competence removed from the Congregation for Clergy and the Roman Rota. Three weeks later, Ratzinger had sent a letter to every bishop in the Catholic world reminding them of the norms and insisting on their implementation.

Pope Benedict's most decisive action was taken in the long-neglected case of Fr. Marcial Maciel, the founder of the immensely wealthy priestly order, the Legionaries of Christ. Complaints and accusations had piled up against Maciel for decades, but the public was hardly prepared for the horrifying reality—the decades-long deception Maciel had perpetrated—that finally emerged. During the pontificate of John Paul II, the Legionaries and Maciel enjoyed the favor of the pope and the support of his powerful secretary of state, Cardinal Angelo Sodano, who had reportedly received enormous sums from the group. In 2004, close to the end of John Paul's pontificate, Ratzinger had ordered the Congregation for the Doctrine of the Faith investigation on Maciel reopened and was ultimately convinced there was substance to the claims of abuse, after his office interviewed more than one hundred former seminarians and priests. Maciel stepped down as head of the Legion only a few days before the death of John Paul II, at whose funeral Cardinal Ratzinger famously decried the "filth" of clerical sex abuse that had grown in the Church.

The investigation continued after Ratzinger was elected pope and in May 2006 the Congregation for the Doctrine of the Faith ordered Maciel to "relinquish any form of public ministry" and to retire to "a reserved life of penitence and prayer." Maciel died in 2008. In the end it came out that the Legion founder had led a double life for decades; addicted to morphine, sexually abusing boys and young men, keeping three mistresses in two countries and fathering six children by them, all sheltered by the order's cult-like devotion to the founder; supported by money donated to the Legion for works of religion.

With the succession of Benedict XVI, even those not inclined to support the "conservative" side in the Church perceived a profound and welcome shift in addressing the scandals. Michael Sean Winters, a columnist at the *National Catholic Reporter*, praised Benedict for focusing on those who had covered for the perpetrators. He called the previous emphasis on the abusers "an utterly ineffectual approach." Abuse of minors, he said, "was horrific" but "what galled, what really gave rise to a sense of betrayal, was that the bishops did not respond to this abuse with the appropriate horror."

"Benedict's willingness to hold bishops accountable is what is needed to mend the church," Winters said. "Pope Benedict gets it. And he has given notice that bishops who don't get it will be replaced." This was confirmed a few days before Benedict's resignation took effect by a senior member of the Vatican's diplomatic corps, Archbishop Miguel Maury Buendia, who said,[19] "This Pope has removed two or three bishops per month throughout the world.... There have been two or three instances in which they said no, and so the Pope simply removed them."

Despite verbal avowals from Pope Francis that he too is a champion against clerical abuse, this reform of accountability appears to have evaporated with Benedict's resignation. In fact, for those paying attention, Francis started signaling the new direction immediately by choosing to honor one of the most notorious of the enabling bishops—namely his electoral ally Cardinal Danneels, who appeared with the new pope on the balcony at St. Peter's Basilica on the night of the election.

Anne Barrett Doyle, the co-director of Bishop Accountability, has remarked: "No other pope has spoken as passionately about the evil of child sex abuse as Francis. No other pope has invoked 'zero tolerance' as often."[20] Yet in the name of his favorite theme, "mercy," Francis decisively broke with the Ratzinger/Benedict program of reform, reducing the penalty for priest abusers to "a lifetime of prayer" and restrictions on celebrating Mass. In February 2017 it was revealed that Francis had "quietly reduced sanctions against a handful of paedophile priests, applying his vision of a merciful church even to its worst offenders.[21]"

A particularly notorious case was Francis' decision to overrule the Congregation for the Doctrine of the Faith's penalties against the Italian priest Mauro Inzoli, who was found guilty in 2012 by an ecclesiastical court of abusing boys as young as twelve and suspended *a divinis*, which barred him from performing priestly duties. Inzoli had especially angered Italians for the brazenness of his behavior—he abused boys in the confessional and convinced them that his molestation was approved by God—and his love of an expensive lifestyle, earning him the nickname "Don Mercedes" in the press.

But in 2014, following an appeal by Inzoli's friends in the Curia, Cardinal Coccopalmerio and Monsignor Vito Pinto, Francis reduced the priest's penalty to a "lifetime of prayer," and a promise to stay away from children, giving him permission to celebrate Mass privately. Francis also ordered him to undergo five years of psychotherapy, a medicalized approach favored by bishops at the height of the sex abuse crisis years and demonstrated to have little effect.

Inzoli's two Curial friends were to become significant figures in later altercations between Francis and his critics within the

College of Cardinals over *Amoris laetitia*, Pope Francis's controversial apostolic exhortation on pastoral matters related to marriage and family life. Cardinal Coccopalmerio, a former auxiliary
bishop to Cardinal Martini, is president of the Pontifical Council for Legislative Texts and Monsignor Pio Vito Pinto now dean
of the Roman Rota.[22] Both these prelates have been key figures
in supporting Francis against the critics of *Amoris laetitia*, who
happen to include Cardinal Müller, the prefect of the Congregation for the Doctrine of the Faith. One journalist has commented:
"Pope Francis, following the advice of his clubby group of allies
in the curia, is pressing to undo the reforms that were instituted
by his predecessors John Paul II and Benedict XVI in handling
cases of abuser priests."[23]

This leniency, however, backfired, and after complaints from
Inzoli's home town of Cremona, police reopened the case against
him. He was tried and convicted, and sentenced to four years,
nine months in prison for "more than a hundred episodes" of
molesting five boys, aged twelve to sixteen. Fifteen other offences
were beyond the statute of limitations. After Inzoli's conviction
in the civil courts, the Vatican belatedly initiated a new canonical trial.

Inzoli's case is not an isolated one. Associated Press reporter
Nicole Winfield wrote that "two canon lawyers and a church
official" told her the pope's emphasis on "mercy" had created
an environment in which "several" priests under canonical sanctions imposed by the Congregation for the Doctrine of the Faith
had appealed successfully to Francis for clemency through powerful Curial connections. The unnamed official noted that such
appeals had rarely been successful with Benedict XVI.

It was rumored that Francis intended to revert competence for sex abuse cases from Cardinal Müller at the Congregation for the Doctrine of the Faith to the Rota and Congregation for Clergy. Instead, Francis merely changed personnel. He summarily removed two Congregation for the Doctrine of the Faith staffers in charge of handling sex abuse cases (declining to give any reasons to Cardinal Müller) and then dismissed Müller himself as prefect of the Congregation for the Doctrine of the Faith in July 2017.

According to the Associated Press's Nicole Winfield, Francis also overruled a request by his own sex abuse commission to create a tribunal of bishops to review sex abuse cases. Perhaps worse, the commission's guidelines for dioceses on handling abuse claims were never sent to the bishops' conferences or even produced on the Vatican's websites.

Francis's new approach of "mercy" and treating sex abuse as a psychological-medical problem, was criticized by a victim-survivor on the sex-abuse advisory commission, Marie Collins, who later resigned, citing a Vatican culture of bureaucratic obstruction and inaction. "All who abuse have made a conscious decision to do so," Collins told the Associated Press. "Even those who are paedophiles, experts will tell you, are still responsible for their actions. They can resist their inclinations."

Questions remain about Bergoglio's knowledge and involvement in the case of decades of sexual abuse of students by priests at the Antonio Provolo Institute, a school for deaf children in Argentina and Verona, Italy. In 2009, twenty-four former students of the institute came forward with horrifying stories of sexual abuse. Pope Benedict's Vatican ordered an investigation, and the diocese of Verona officially apologized to the Italian victims, but the Vatican has taken no action since, even though the students sent a letter to Francis in 2014, asking him for an investigative commission. The only response the group ever received from Rome was a note from Archbishop Angelo Becciu, who said the request for a commission had been passed on to the Italian bishops' conference. In 2016, two of the priests involved, Nicola Corradi and Horacio Corbacho, were arrested in Argentina. The Provolo Association representing the victims told the Associated Press after the arrests that the Vatican had still done nothing and raised questions about Francis himself. "We have to ask ourselves: the Pope, who was for many years the primate of the Argentine church, did he know nothing about clerical abuse in his country?" A canon lawyer for the group, Carlos Lombardi, told the press, "Either he lives outside of reality or this is enormously cynical...it's a mockery."[24]

The pope has outraged even his most faithful admirers in yet another sexual abuse case, this one involving Bishop Juan Barros of Chile. On January 23, 2018, the *National Catholic Reporter*, hitherto a bastion of Francis loyalism, carried an editorial proclaiming: "Pope Francis's defense of Chilean Bishop Juan Barros Madrid is only the latest in a number of statements he has made in his nearly five-year papacy that have hurt survivors, and the whole body of the church."[25] The article went on: "Within the space of four days, Pope Francis twice slandered abuse survivors. On the papal flight from Peru Jan. 21, he again called testimony against Chilean bishop Juan Barros Madrid 'calumny.' Despite at least three survivors' public accounts to the contrary, he also again said he had not seen evidence of Barros' involvement in a cover-up to protect notorious abuser Fr. Fernando Karadima. These remarks are at least shameful. At the most, they suggest that Francis now could be complicit in the cover-up.... The pope's statements on zero tolerance have been strong, but again and again he has refused to deal decisively with those who provided cover for the abusers.... In a bluntly critical statement, the likes of which we have struggled to find parallel in recent church history, Boston Cardinal Seán O'Malley said the pope's slander against survivors has caused them 'great pain.'... When it comes to confronting the clericalism that is the foundation for abuse scandal, the pope's stony countenance is part of the problem."

When Pope Francis's friends start making remarks like that, a wheel has come off the Francis bandwagon. Matters got worse, when it was revealed in February 2018 that despite Francis's insistence that he had seen no evidence of victims coming forward to accuse Bishop Juan Barros of a cover-up, apparently Cardinal Seán O'Malley had in fact handed him an eight-page letter by a victim alleging just that—that Bishop Juan Barros had not only covered up sexual abuse but was an eyewitness to it. A copy of a letter was acquired by the Associated Press.

To say the least, Pope Francis has not held the "zero tolerance" line of Pope Benedict when it comes to clerical sexual abuse and has been far more lenient, or irresponsible, in dealing with this ongoing moral scandal within the Church.

What Happened to the Reform of the Vatican Finances?

It is not surprising that the worst instances of corruption in the Curia have always occurred in the departments that manage money, both because of the personal temptations of wealth and because the officials in those departments, being ignorant of the business and financial worlds, were in constant danger of being drawn into methods of investment and finance that were either dubious or outright illegal. The criminal charges to which Archbishop Marcinkus and Bishop de Bonis exposed themselves in the 1980s and 1990s should have been warnings about the need for reform, but those warnings apparently went unheeded in the Vatican, where, if anything, the culture of avarice and dishonesty seemed to get worse.

A glaring example emerged just three months into the reign of Pope Francis. Monsignor Nunzio Scarano, the chief accountant at the Administration of the Patrimony of the Apostolic See (*Amministrazione del Patrimonio della Sede Apostolica* or APSA), was arrested in June 2013 on a charge of trying to smuggle twenty-two million euros from Switzerland into Italy in a private jet. It transpired that Monsignor Scarano had for years been living a life of luxury funded by his Vatican appointment. He lived in a seventeen-room apartment in Salerno filled with works of art, including van Gogh and Chagall, and was known as "Monsignor 500" for the five-hundred-euro notes in which he famously made his transactions.

As an accomplice in his cash-smuggling plan, Monsignor Scarano made the mistake of picking an agent of the Italian secret service, Giovanni Mario Zito, to whom he paid 217,000 euros. When Zito disclosed the plot to the authorities, Scarano denied culpability and accused Zito of having stolen the 217,000 euros from him. At Scarano's trial in January 2016, he was convicted of defamation for the accusation he had made against Zito, but was found not guilty of currency smuggling because the plot unraveled before it was carried out.[26]

The Scarano case was explosive not only because of the immediate charges, but because Monsignor Scarano accused his colleagues in the Vatican of widespread financial wrongdoing. He revealed that officials at APSA routinely accepted gifts from banks looking to attract the Vatican's money—these gifts included trips, five-star hotels, and massages. Those officials made a practice of transferring funds frequently from one bank to another, partly in order to keep the benefits flowing. Monsignor Scarano also said that APSA officials rigged the awarding of contracts that were supposedly up for competitive bidding.[27]

When Pope Francis took power, Benedict XVI had already begun the process of reform: he created the Financial Information Authority to ensure transparency of the Vatican's financial transactions, and he took the decision to call in Moneyval, the Council of Europe's agency against money-laundering, to audit the Curia's financial bodies, thus subjecting the Vatican to the first outside inspection in its history. Things might have rested there, but the Scarano revelations were probably the trigger for a more far-reaching review.

In July 2013, Pope Francis set up a pontifical commission, employing major consultancy firms, to analyze and suggest reforms of the Curia's economic institutions (the *Pontificia Commissione Referente di Studio e di Indirizzo sull'Organizzazione della Struttura Economica-Amministrativa della Santa Sede*). Chief among these economic institutions is the Administration of the Patrimony of the Apostolic See, which is the treasury and general accounting department of the Vatican. Before 2014, when it was reorganized, it had an "ordinary section," responsible for administering (and purchasing) the property holdings of the Holy See, and an "extraordinary section" which oversaw a large investment portfolio. There is also the Istituto per le Opere di Religione (IOR), popularly known as the "Vatican Bank." It manages accounts for individuals or groups or organizations connected with the Vatican, but an investigation in 2013 showed that a large number of accounts were held by people outside the Vatican, presumably for the purposes of tax evasion. Thousands of accounts were abruptly closed at this time. In July 2013 the head of IOR, Ernst von Freyberg, publicly admitted that money-laundering was among the activities that lax control had permitted to take place, and he named Monsignor Scarano as "a real professional in money-laundering." Finally, there is the governorate of the Vatican City State, which controls the large sums of money flowing from the museums, shops, and supermarkets of Vatican City.

Over and above these was the Secretariat of State, which had in the past half-century increased its power and authority over all Curial departments. In particular, Cardinal Bertone, as part of his empire-building between 2006 and 2013, had taken care to establish control of every aspect of Vatican finances. Departments of special relevance were the Prefecture of Economic Affairs of the Holy See (whose responsibilities were to be taken over by the new Secretariat for the Economy in 2015), the Congregation of Propaganda Fide, which has an enormous budget, and the Congregation for the Causes of Saints, because of the large sums that flow in to fund the processes of beatification and canonization—an activity that became big business with the increase in such processes under John Paul II.

By February 2014, Pope Francis's reform commission had discovered, amongst other things, that the Secretariat of State held ninety-four million euros unaccounted for in its financial statements.[28] Such lax accounting gave force to recommendations for comprehensive reform of the Vatican's financial structures. As an overall supervising body, the commission recommended the creation of a Council for the Economy, with an international membership of eight prelates and seven lay people, to meet every two months. The most radical structural reform was the creation of a Secretariat for the Economy, with very wide powers. It was to be on equal footing with the Secretariat of State, reporting directly to the pope, and it was to take over extensive responsibilities hitherto resting with other bodies. It would absorb the Prefecture of Economic Affairs and would take over from APSA the whole of its "ordinary section," the management of real estate and personnel. Even more ambitious, it would assume the financial and human-resources responsibilities of the Secretariat of State—part of a comprehensive cutting down of the latter's power that was being proposed at the time.

But the cardinals at the heart of the Curia were too powerful to permit such an upheaval. Cardinal Parolin, whom Pope Francis had made secretary of state in October 2013, fought hard for the interests of his over-mighty office. The myth of Pope Francis as a radical reformer brushing aside vested interests is disproved by what happened next. What could have been easier than to accept a plan made on the recommendations of eminent consultancy firms—KPMG, McKinsey & Co., Ernst & Young, Promontory Financial Group—with a recognized competence to advise on efficiency and transparency? But Pope Francis allowed a clique of cardinals to hamstring the reform from the start. Its main lines were put in place—the creation of the Council and the Secretariat for the Economy—but significant parts were discarded. For example, it had been pointed out that a purely administrative body such as APSA did not need to have a cardinal at its head; but this perquisite was too valuable to be given up, and APSA continues to be headed by a cardinal (Domenico Calcagno, whose doings will be inspected shortly). APSA did not give up its management of real estate to the Secretariat for the Economy, though it handed over the control of the rental income. The governorate and the Congregation of Propaganda remained autonomous. The Secretariat of State resisted all attempts to cut it down, and in the financial field it retained control of "Peter's Pence," the donations made to the Holy See by the faithful all over the world, bringing in more than fifty million euros a year.[29]

The Australian Cardinal George Pell, who had the reputation of a tough administrator, was made head of the Secretariat for the Economy in February 2014, with a mandate for five years. With his ally the French layman Jean-Baptiste de Franssu in charge of IOR, Pell quickly began to make an impact on Vatican affairs. Within months, the outspoken cardinal announced that he had found 936 million euros in the various Vatican dicasteries which had not been entered in the balance sheets, and by February 2015 the figure had been raised to 1.4 billion.[30] These revelations—and Cardinal Pell's blunt, honest, undiplomatic style—did not make him popular with the officials around him.

The opposition to Cardinal Pell has been headed by four cardinals who are interested not merely in stalling the financial reform but returning the Vatican structures to the position before Pell appeared on the scene. We may begin with Cardinal Domenico Calcagno, who has been president of APSA since 2011 and who is the most scandalous of the four. Gianluigi Nuzzi, in one of his more outspoken comments, describes Calcagno as "the scheming prelate and wily connoisseur of the Curia's secrets."[31] Before being appointed to the Curia, Calcagno had been bishop of Savona, where between 2002 and 2003 he ignored repeated instances of sexual violence against minors by one of his priests, simply moving him on to another parish. Calcagno is still under investigation for real-estate dealings that harmed the diocese's finances.[32] It is a commentary on Francis's pontificate that such a background is not thought incompatible with the holding of one of the key financial posts in the Vatican.

Another of Pell's opponents is Cardinal Giuseppe Versaldi, who was president of the Prefecture of Economic Affairs from 2011 to 2015. In 2014 Cardinal Versaldi was caught in an intercepted telephone call advising the head of the Vatican's Bambino Gesù Hospital to keep from the pope the news that thirty million euros of the hospital's funds had been misappropriated.[33] The response to this discovery, a year into Pope Francis's papacy, was revealingly mild. Cardinal Versaldi lost the Prefecture of Economic Affairs but was rewarded by being made prefect of the Congregation for Catholic Education, the position he still holds. As an ally of Cardinal Calcagno, he is sparing no effort to recover his former power.

The third cardinal to be noticed is Giuseppe Bertello, the president of the governorate of the Vatican City State, whose lack of enthusiasm for transparency was seen in the early stages of the reform efforts. Journalist Gianluigi Nuzzi has described in his book

Merchants in the Temple how Cardinal Bertello and his secretary general tried to stonewall the reform Commission's requests for financial information.[34] What Calcagno, Versaldi, and Bertello have in common was that they were all brought into the Vatican by Cardinal Bertone when he was secretary of state. This association was thought toxic in the first stages of Francis's pontificate, and it was assumed that their heads would soon roll. In fact, they are still in power and have shown an extraordinary resilience.

Above these three is the secretary of state, Cardinal Pietro Parolin, who has put up a well-documented resistance to Pope Francis's supposed new regime of transparency.[35] But his main characteristic is his determination not to give up an ounce of his enormous power. In that cause, he immediately identified Cardinal Pell as the chief enemy, and he has devoted himself in the past three years to stalling Pell's efforts at reform and clipping his power. In this, Pope Francis has given him a free hand, repeatedly granting his demands to chip away at the new financial structure that seemed to be put in place in 2014.

It is worth noting that none of the four cardinals mentioned can be viewed as representing a Curialist caste devoted to preserving control against a reforming pope. All of them came to their posts quite recently, Cardinals Calcagno, Versaldi, and Bertello having been installed by the Secretary of State Bertone in the same year, 2011, while Cardinal Parolin was appointed by Pope Francis himself in 2013. What they are fighting for is not a traditional system of government but one which came into its present form, with all its abuses, in very modern times.

The key to the reversal of the reform that was designed in 2014 lies in the contrast in political savvy between Cardinal Pell and the four cardinals who confronted him. As an Anglo-Saxon, Cardinal Pell has all the assumptions of a man from a parliamentary culture: the reform had been decreed by legal authority, officials would obviously respect the policy and work to carry it out, and all that remained to do was to get on with it. But Cardinals Parolin, Calcagno, Versaldi, and Bertello are Italians, and they know there is often a wide difference between what an administration says it will do and what it intends to do. Above all, the historic lessons of the Italian princely courts, not least the papal court, is in the marrow of their bones. In that world, results were not achieved by debate and administrative resolutions, they were gained by having the ear of the monarch, attending him day by day, and dropping plausible advice constantly into his ear. That is the path which they have very successfully followed, and it is why Cardinal Calcagno has, over the last four years, been able to regain much of the power that reform was supposed to strip from him and APSA.

While media attention was being focused on IOR (understandably, in view of its past misdeeds), it was not noticed that APSA itself has been operating as a parallel "Vatican Bank," and it has escaped the reforms to which IOR has been subject. APSA has long been managing accounts for private customers and opening coded accounts for them in Swiss banks (it is not known whether it is still going on). This has been a favorite resource for rich Italians, allowing them to put money into investment funds and avoid paying tax. In these services, APSA has acted in competition with IOR in its quest for customers, with officials being known to assure investors that APSA would outperform IOR. There is reason to believe that all along it has been APSA rather than IOR that was the real factory of criminality in the Vatican finances.[36] Under Cardinal Calcagno, APSA has shrugged off the attempted reforms with insolent ease, while it has also defied the new economic rules by engaging expensive consultants and lawyers to help hide its murky past. As for Pope Francis, he has repeatedly been made aware of all this but has taken no action.

Dishonesty, or at least a large helping of incompetence, was the ingredient in the next financial scandal that emerged in 2016. Some fifteen years ago, the management of the large real-estate holdings of the Basilica of St. Peter was taken away from the Canons of St. Peter and transferred to APSA. The portfolio included some three hundred properties, mainly in central Rome and often of great historic value. In 2016 it was found that about eighty of the apartments concerned had simply been left derelict. Many of the others were let at absurdly cheap rents, or the rents had been left unpaid or uncollected. Sometimes preferential rents are a legitimate way to ensure that Church employees will have accommodation in Rome, but often they are personal favors with no official justification. The result was that the income of this rich patrimony had been turned into a seven-hundred-thousand-euro deficit, and the Canons of St. Peter were told in 2016 that they could not elect any new members because there were no funds to pay them.[37]

This is just one aspect of the regime that prevails at APSA. Cardinal Pell has repeatedly asked the pope for Cardinal Calcagno's dismissal, and Francis has replied that he will dismiss him if proof of wrongdoing is shown to him. In fact, proof after proof has been submitted but Calcagno continues to be protected. He knows how to keep in favor, and for a long time was dining with the pope nearly every night. In his war against Cardinal Pell,

Cardinal Calcagno has been steadily winning; he has even recovered for APSA the supervision of the Vatican's financial assets that had been transferred to the Secretariat for the Economy.

The drive against corruption in the Vatican has thus been reduced to a mockery. The most telling sign is the fact that until late 2017 not a single prosecution for financial crime took place in the Tribunal of the Vatican City State under Pope Francis. The Vatican's watchdog agency, the Financial Information Authority, had referred seventeen reports to the Office of the Promoter of Justice, but none of them had resulted in a prosecution, let alone a conviction. We may contrast this with the fate of Monsignor Lucio Vallejo, the former secretary of the Prefecture for Economic Affairs. He was tried in the summer of 2016 and sentenced to eighteen months in prison (which he served in the Vatican's own cells) for having released secret documents to journalist Gianluigi Nuzzi with the intention of exposing how the alleged reforms of the Vatican's financial systems were flawed, and reform was not being carried out. (His accomplice Francesca Chaouqui was given a ten-month suspended sentence.)[38]

An early sign that attempted financial reforms were being reversed was the fate of the comprehensive audit that was introduced by Cardinal Pell. In December 2015 it was decreed that PricewaterhouseCoopers would be conducting an outside audit of all the Vatican's financial bodies, and this began straight away. After four months, however, its suspension was announced, without reasons being given,[39] and in June 2016 it was officially canceled. The move came from Cardinal Parolin himself, whose *sostituto*, Archbishop Becciu, telephoned PricewaterhouseCoopers to inform them that the audit would not be applied to the Secretariat of State, thus making it virtually pointless.

Even before the beginning of the audit, in October 2014, the Secretariat of State had recovered some of its authority that had been transferred to the Secretariat for the Economy. In July 2016, the pope signed a *motu proprio* that reduced the Secretariat for the Economy to a supervisory role, stripping it of its former wide powers.[40] The *Wall Street Journal* described this as "a sign that the Vatican's established interests have gained the Pope's support."[41] The Secretariat for the Economy had not been notified in advance of the *motu proprio*, just as it had not been consulted about the cancelation of the PricewaterhouseCoopers audit. It was a clear signal that the Secretariat of State was back in control and was not observing amenities. In fact, the reality is far worse. The Secretariat for the Economy has now been left virtually empty, and many of its nominal staff are in fact subject to APSA, to which they owe their real loyalty. Having recovered its control of human resources, the Secretariat of State uses that power to ensure that jobs under Cardinal Pell are only on short-term contracts and without the security and generous benefits that apply in the Secretariat of State and APSA.

Do these facts indicate that Pope Francis is against financial reform in itself? That seems an unjustified conclusion, but from his point of view it comes a long way behind the power games that are at the heart of his governing style. George Pell falls into a class of prelates—Cardinals Burke and Müller are other leading examples—who have earned Francis's dislike because of their independence and their refusal to fall into the role of pawns. Cardinal Pell has been in the habit of speaking his mind to the pope on a variety of subjects, not only financial, and he has never been impressed with Francis's record as a reformer. Looking at such things as the financial and administrative reform of the Curia, or the drive against sex-offending priests, Pell has commented: "Francis is the opposite of Theodore Roosevelt. He talks loud and carries a small stick." Pope Francis does not like having such strong, independent truth-tellers around him, especially in positions of power, but neither is it his style to hit at such figures directly, particularly when, in the case of Pell, he appointed him to lead the cause of reform. The apt comment has been made: "Rather than pulling a nail, Pope Francis finds another tool."[42] And the tools he prefers to Pell are Cardinal Calcagno, who is beholden to him for the restoration of his power, and Cardinal Parolin, who as secretary of state has implemented and consented to all the tyrannical measures of his pontificate.

Pope Francis might have hoped that Cardinal Pell would have been more beholden to him as well, because Pell, as a bishop in Australia, was accused of failing to take sufficient and effective action against cases of sexual abuse among his clergy. Pell admitted to making mistakes, at a time when awareness of the problem was less acute than it is today, and while it is not the purpose of this book to present Cardinal Pell as a hero, it may be that a lack of sensitivity in his character was responsible for his failures. More recently he has been accused of molesting boys himself, in allegations which relate to incidents from forty years ago and which he denied from the moment they were made. Before it was known whether the Australian authorities would prosecute, it was noted that the accusations were of such minor offences that if this had been an ordinary case it would have been dropped some time ago, and one Australian politician, Amanda Vanstone, has opined on the subject: "What we are seeing is no better than a lynch mob from the dark ages."[43] The decision to prosecute was taken in June 2017, and Cardinal Pell has returned to Australia to stand trial. There are those who think that Pell's enemies both in Australia and in the Vatican have been using these allegations, and prosecution, to weaken him politically within the Church.

If so, the scheme has a certain weakness. Firstly, Cardinal Pell has not been asked to resign his Vatican appointment, as his enemies would have hoped. Secondly, it seems rather unlikely that he will be found guilty, even in a first trial, let alone on appeal. This means that he will probably one day return to Rome and take up the cudgels again. If he does, his Curial opponents (with at least the tacit approval of Pope Francis) will try to limit his authority as much as possible, and wait until the expiry of his five-year mandate. Then, they will return to business as usual, and blame the failure of the financial reforms on Pell.

One may be permitted, however, to point out a hitch to this plan: Pope Francis will not live forever. There is always the danger that the next pope will be a genuine reformer, that he will order an investigation of what has been going on in the Vatican, and then the world will discover how the reform we were promised has been thoroughly falsified. People will assess what it means that three cardinals who had been assumed to be on their way out in 2013 are now very much back in, and that a declared intention to cut down the power of the Secretariat of State has resulted in a situation in which the secretariat is more powerful and arbitrary than ever.

The details of the failure of the Vatican's financial reform are known to journalists who have been studying the subject: they are given in the numerous articles that have been cited in the course of this chapter. But the general lessons have yet to be drawn. A proper indictment has been obscured by an outsiders' idea that a reforming pope is being opposed by "conservatives" in the Curia when, in fact, inside the Curia, everyone knows exactly who Cardinal Pell's enemies are and that they derive their power from the favor shown to them by Pope Francis.

Open War

The conflict between the Secretariat for the Economy and APSA entered a new and violent phase in May 2017 when a missive was distributed from APSA to Vatican departments, instructing them to provide financial information for an audit by Pricewater-houseCoopers that was to take place under APSA's direction—the very measure that had been blocked when it was tried by the Secretariat for the Economy. Monsignor Rivella, who was responsible for the letter, claimed that the Council for the Economy had authorized APSA to do this, a statement that was soon found to be untrue. Within days, Cardinal Pell and the auditor general sent letters to the departments concerned countermanding the order and stating that APSA was exceeding its authority.[44]

The winner of this battle was soon revealed: on June 20, 2017, the "resignation" was announced of the auditor general, Libero Milone,[45] allegedly because he refused to accept a reduction in his salary. On September 24, Milone publicly revealed the circumstances of his dismissal.[46] Milone said that on the morning of June 19, Archbishop Becciu ordered him to resign in a private interview, stating that complaints had been made against him, that he had exceeded his authority and misused funds, and that the order for his resignation came from Pope Francis himself. Despite the protests of Mr. Milone that the complaints against him were fabricated, the dismissal went ahead in the style of a totalitarian state: on the same day, Vatican Police raided the auditor general's office, accompanied by members of the Vatican Fire Department. They detained and interrogated Mr. Milone for hours, often shouting at him, and seized his phones, computers, and files. The police then broke into the office of the deputy auditor general, Ferruccio Pannico, using axes, crowbars, hammers, and chisels, even though they had the keys available to them. Mr. Pannico, who was absent from the office, was forced to resign the next day. All people in the office of the auditor general, employees and visitors, were detained, temporarily deprived of their cell phones, and interrogated. Milone's and Pannico's resignations came as the result of an ultimatum: resign or be arrested. They were obliged to sign nondisclosure agreements, which limited what Mr. Milone could say in his interview of September 24, but he revealed that the accusations against him started with a "complaint" that he had called in a company from outside the Vatican when he found that his computer had been tampered with. The consultants found that his computer had been the target of an unauthorized access, while his secretary's computer had been infected with spyware that copied files. When Mr. Milone made his disclosures on September 24, Archbishop Becciu retaliated vehemently, denying his accusations, and stating that the reason for the dismissal was that Milone (the official, let us remember, who had been appointed to search out financial wrongdoing in the Vatican) had been "spying" on his superiors and staff, including Becciu himself. This is indeed rich, coming from an organization which has taken internal espionage to a level unknown since Ceausescu's Romania.[47]

As to the real cause of Mr. Milone's dismissal, it was soon being said that he was getting too close to the finances of the Secretariat of State. One body whose privacy his researches threatened was Centesimus Annus, an under-examined foundation which is supposed to be a center for Church fundraising but which was named by Moneyval in 2012 as controlling a large slice of the Vatican's wealth. Even more sensitively, Milone may have been getting close to confirming the allegation that Peter's Pence—the donations of the faithful to the Holy See—had been diverted to aid the funding of Hillary Clinton's presidential campaign in 2016.

The timing of the blow was also significant, and it relates to the announcement made public a few days later that Cardinal Pell was going to be charged with child-molestation by the Australian police. On June 19, only the Secretariat of State knew this in Rome, through its nuncio in Australia, while the Vatican Press Office made the announcement, with unnecessary panoply, ten days later. The conclusion to be drawn is that, with Pell thus neutralized, the Secretariat of State felt that it was safe to get rid of his chief ally, and assumed that the scandal of firing Milone would soon be overshadowed by the sex-abuse allegations leveled against Cardinal Pell.

The personal responsibility of Pope Francis for this political maneuver admits of little doubt. Archbishop Becciu assured Milone on June 19 that the order for his dismissal came from the pope, and there is little reason to doubt it: it falls within the pattern of the many defenestrations ordered by Jorge Bergoglio, behind the scenes, during the course of his career. In his interview of September 24, Milone revealed that following his dismissal he wrote a letter to the pope, through a secure channel, denouncing the injustice and protesting that he was the victim of "*una montatura*" (a setup). He never received a reply, nor has he been successful in his efforts to speak personally to Pope Francis.

The role played in this affair by the Vatican's Promoter of Justice, its chief prosecutor, also requires comment. While the Vatican bragged in January 2017 that it would be prosecuting financial crimes for the first time, the Promoter of Justice's draconian approach with Mr. Milone contrasts with his sluggish, if not craven, policy in dealing with the numerous cases of financial crimes reported to his office. The paralysis of the justice system in the Vatican remains cause for major concern.

Other questions still remain about the Milone case. For instance, did the Vatican Police overstep their bounds by conducting their raid on the auditor general's office, which is located outside of Vatican City? Was the raid, and the seizure of files, conducted to protect powerful persons from charges of corruption? How committed to reform can Pope Francis be if he punishes or dismisses or sidelines those charged with ferreting out corruption and leaves power, or restores power, to the administrators who oversaw corrupt departments in the first place?

On November 27, 2017, Giulio Mattietti, the assistant director of IOR, was dismissed with the same abruptness as Libero Milone had been, after an accusation of "administrative offences."[48] Mattietti had been appointed by Pope Francis just two years earlier, and it adds to the impression that attempts at Vatican financial reform are being reversed—a case of chaotic mismanagement if nothing else. Here at least the effects of Pope Francis's philosophy of "creating a mess" are being shown in abundance.

To sum up: four vitally important reformist bodies were put in place in the last few years, the Financial Information Authority, the Council for the Economy, the Secretariat for the Economy, and the Office of the Auditor General. Since their inception, these entities have been the target of attacks by anti-reform members of the Curia, left in place and empowered by Pope Francis himself—attacks that have made these reformist bodies effectively powerless. Was the pope aware of these attacks? Insiders confirm to us that the answer is yes, and that he signed one illogical executive order after another to accelerate the demise of these bodies. If this is the case, Pope Francis might be storing up more trouble than he imagines, because if the Vatican fails to reform itself, secular authorities might well step in.

How long, for example, will the Italian judiciary wait before demanding the names of the Italian citizens who have broken Italian law, in acts from money laundering to tax evasion, by using APSA-ciphered accounts? Will European and international banking authorities decide to shut down APSA's access to global banking until APSA is reformed by bodies outside the Vatican? And finally, and most historic of all, will Francis's failures prompt the Italian government to denounce the Lateran Treaty of 1929, ending Vatican City's status as an independent state, in order to clean up the lawless, corrupt playground the Vatican has become?

Chapter 4

BEATING A NEW (CROOKED) PATH

1. THE SYNODS ON THE FAMILY: A NEW APPROACH TO SEXUAL MORALITY

On October 8, 2013, Pope Francis announced that two synods would be held to discuss challenges facing the family. The first, the Extraordinary Synod, would be held October 2014 and the second, the Ordinary Synod, October 2015.

The period leading up to the synods was dominated by the proposal, spearheaded by Cardinal Walter Kasper, that Catholics who had divorced and entered into invalid civil unions could be admitted to the sacraments of Penance and Holy Communion without amendment of life. Kasper had been pursuing this goal for many years. In September 1993 he and two other German bishops had issued a pastoral letter calling for permission for this practice in certain cases. The Congregation for the Doctrine of the Faith responded by restating the Church's traditional teaching, as upheld in the 1981 apostolic exhortation *Familiaris consortio*.

Cardinal Kasper was brought to renewed prominence at the first Angelus address of the new pope, on March 17, 2013, when Francis praised Kasper's book *Mercy: The Essence of the Gospel and the Key to Christian Life*, one of the earliest confirmations that Pope Francis intended to steer the Church in a "progressive" direction.

The organization of the synods on the family was in the hands of the synod secretariat headed by Cardinal Lorenzo Baldisseri. On October 26, 2013, the secretariat sent a questionnaire to all bishops' conferences inviting responses to questions relating to marriage, the family, and sexual ethics, with a focus on irregular unions. Just three days earlier Cardinal Gerhard Müller, prefect of the Congregation for the Doctrine of the Faith, had published an article in *L'Osservatore Romano* explaining why it was impossible for there to be any change to Church teaching on the admission of the divorced and remarried to the sacraments.[1] He was clearly concerned about the direction of the synod, even before the official consultation exercise had been launched.

Cardinal Müller's fears seemed to be justified when, on November 7, 2013, Cardinal Reinhard Marx, a member of Pope Francis's inner council of nine cardinals, responded that Müller wouldn't be able to "stop the debate."[2] Cardinal Kasper was invited to give an address at the consistory of cardinals held on February 20, 2014, and he used the opportunity to explain his proposal at length. He was the only cardinal present who was given such an opportunity. It was reported that around four-fifths of the cardinals present spoke against his position.[3] Kasper responded to the hostile reaction by stressing that he was acting for the pope. He thanked "the Holy Father for his friendly words and for his confidence in having entrusted me with this report."[4]

Fr. Federico Lombardi, the Holy See press officer, told the media that the pope had called on the cardinals to deal with the problems facing the family without "casuistry" and that Kasper's speech was "in great harmony" with the words of the pope.[5] The next day the pope lavished praise on Kasper: "Yesterday, before falling asleep, though not to fall asleep, I read, or re-read, Cardinal Kasper's remarks. I would like to thank him, because I found a deep theology; and serene thoughts in theology. It is nice to read serene theology. It did me well and I had an idea, and excuse me if I embarrass your Eminence, but the idea is: this is called doing theology while kneeling. Thank you. Thank you."[6]

Kasper's speech was published a few weeks later with the pope's words of praise on the back cover. Around the same time a collection of extracts from homilies of Pope Francis was published under the title *The Church of Mercy*. The foreword was written by the archbishop of Westminster, Cardinal Vincent Nichols, something of a dissenter from Catholic teaching on sexual ethics.[7] Nichols's retired predecessor at Westminster, Cardinal Murphy-O'Connor, a member of the St. Gallen Group and an active campaigner for the election of Cardinal Bergoglio, told *Vatican Insider* in March 2014, "when the cardinals elected Bergoglio they did not know what a Pandora's box they were opening, they did not know what a steely character he was, they

did not know that he was a Jesuit in very deep ways, they did not
know who they were electing."[8]

Between February and October 2014 Kasper advocated for
his proposal, traveling to the United States and giving media
interviews. Yet the opposition within the College of Cardinals
was formidable. Five cardinals, Walter Brandmüller, Raymond
Burke, Carlo Caffarra, Gerhard Müller, and Velasio de Paolis
contributed, with four other scholars, to a comprehensive reply
to Kasper's arguments published in book form as *Remaining in
the Truth of Christ: Marriage and Communion in the Catholic
Church*. There are indications that the response discomfited both
Cardinal Kasper and the pope. *La Croix* reported that the Holy
Father was said to be "displeased" by those cardinals who had
made contributions to *Remaining in the Truth of Christ*. It also
reported that he "demanded" that Cardinal Müller should not
take part in promoting the book.[9]

On September 18, 2014, Kasper told *Il Mattino*: "I agreed
upon everything with him. He was in agreement. What can a
cardinal do, except be with the Pope? I am not the target, the
target is another one.... They know that I have not done these
things by myself. I agreed with the Pope, I spoke twice with him.
He showed himself content. Now, they create this controversy.
A Cardinal must be close to the Pope, by his side. The Cardinals
are the Pope's co-operators."[10]

Perhaps the most striking revelation of the immediate pre-
synod period was that made public on September 20 by Marco
Tosatti of *La Stampa*. He revealed that Cardinal Baldisseri, secretary of the General Synod of Bishops, had been heard explaining
how the Extraordinary Synod was going to be managed in order

to achieve the secretariat's desired results. This would be done in three ways; the first, which had already been accomplished, was that all interventions by synod fathers had to be submitted by September 8. This made possible the second strategy, which was to read all the interventions carefully to ensure that any points contrary to the desired agenda could be answered in the most effective way possible before the speaker had the chance to speak. The third strategy was simply to prevent certain synod fathers from even addressing the assembly. They would be told that there was no more time for interventions but that their views would be taken into account in the final report. Tosatti's revelation alerted participants and commentators to the threat of manipulation. At a pre-synod press conference on October 3, Cardinal Baldisseri became angry as journalists questioned the lack of transparency: "you should come up here if you know everything, maybe you should be a synod father," he snapped at a female reporter.[11]

Getting the Desired Result

The Extraordinary Synod began on October 5, 2014, with an opening sermon from Pope Francis condemning "evil pastors" who "lay intolerable burdens on the shoulders of others, which they themselves do not lift a finger to move." "Synod Assemblies," he continued, "are not meant to discuss beautiful and clever ideas, or to see who is more intelligent."[12]

Concerns that this was an attempt to intimidate synod fathers were strengthened by an interview given by the Holy Father to the Argentinian newspaper *La Nación*, which was published two days after his sermon. The pope was asked by the interviewer if he was "worried" about the book *Remaining in the Truth of Christ*. In his reply Francis distinguished himself from its authors by stating that he enjoyed "debating with the very conservative, but intellectually well-formed bishops." But, he said, "the world has changed and the Church cannot lock itself into alleged interpretations of dogma."[13]

During the first week of the assembly each synod father was given four minutes to speak in the plenary sessions. For the first time in the history of the modern synod neither the texts of the speeches nor detailed summaries were published; instead the Vatican press officers simply gave brief overviews of what had been said taken from their own handwritten notes. It quickly became apparent that these summaries gave an unbalanced impression of the interventions. Fr. Rosica, the English-speaking spokesman, attracted particular criticism because of the perceived bias of his summaries. For example, Rosica proffered his view that "one of the salient interventions" of the day was the suggestion that there was a great desire for our language "to change in order to meet the concrete situations," and that "'living in sin,' 'intrinsically disordered,' or 'contraceptive mentality,' are not necessarily words that invite people to draw closer to Christ and the Church." Yet it was far from clear that interventions of this kind were typical. A senior Vatican official told journalist Edward Pentin, "Almost all of Rosica's and Lombardi's briefings were geared toward spinning a liberal angle," while speeches "in favour of tradition were not reported."[14]

Marco Tossatti reflected that while in previous synods you could know what every single bishop had said, during the current assembly "you had nothing of this, you had just a vague *'riassunto,'* or summary ... You couldn't know what everyone said about the issues."[15] Cardinal Müller was among those who spoke out against the new procedures. He insisted that "all Christians have the right to be informed about the intervention of their bishops."[16] Cardinal Burke told *Il Foglio*: "it seems to me that something is not working well if the information is manipulated in a way so as to stress only one position instead of reporting faithfully the various positions that were expressed. This worries me very much, because a consistent number of bishops do not accept the idea of a break with traditional Church teaching, but few know this."[17]

Perhaps the most notorious evidence of manipulation was the *Relatio post disceptationem,* which was presented to both the synod fathers and the press on October 13. This controversial document, purported to be based on the interventions of the synod fathers, emphasized the Church's openness to the "Kasper Proposal," the need for the Church to "value" the homosexual orientation of individuals, and the need for the Church to focus on the supposedly positive elements of sinful unions, such as cohabitation.

Voices of Dissent

The report was hailed as a revolution in the Church by many in the media despite the insistence of many synod fathers that it was not an accurate reflection of the interventions made. Cardinal Napier, one of the fifteen members of the permanent council of the synod, recalled synod fathers asking, "How then could this be stated as coming from the synod when the synod hasn't even discussed it yet?" and others stating, "there are things said there about the synod saying this, that, and the other, but nobody ever said them." Napier concluded: "So that's when it became plain that there was some engineering going on."[18] He had been warned about this potential threat. A few months before the synod began, one of those associated with the synod had told Napier that he was "very disturbed" by what he had been witnessing. "It amounted to manipulating the synod, engineering it in a certain direction," Napier recalled. "I asked: 'But why?' He said: 'Because they want a certain result.'"[19]

Cardinal Pell, prefect of the Secretariat for the Economy, responded to the *Relatio* by alleging that "radical elements" were using proposals for the reception of Holy Communion by the remarried as a "stalking horse" for further changes in the Church's teaching on questions of sexual morality. The report was, he said, "tendentious, skewed; it didn't represent accurately the feelings of the synod fathers .... In the immediate reaction to it, when there was an hour, an hour-and-a-half of discussion, three-quarters of those who spoke had some problems with the document," Pell remarked.[20]

Cardinal Burke told *Catholic World Report*: "I wholeheartedly agree with what Cardinal George Pell and Cardinal Wilfrid Fox Napier have stated regarding the manipulation of the Synod Fathers by means of the *Relatio post disceptationem*. It is clear that whoever wrote the *Relatio* has an agenda and simply used the authority of a solemn meeting of Cardinals and Bishops to advance his agenda without respect for the discussion which took place during the first week of the Synod."[21]

Cardinal Baldisseri would later confirm that this document, and all the other synodal documents, had received the approval of Pope Francis before their publication: "Pay attention, as this is something one really should know.... The pope presided over all of the council meetings of the secretariat. He presides. I am the secretary. And so the documents were all seen and approved by the pope, with the approval of his presence. Even the documents during the synod, such as the *Relatio ante disceptationem,* the *Relatio post disceptationem,* and the *Relatio synodi* were seen by him before they were published."[22]

Pope Francis may have approved the *Relatio* but Cardinal Erdo, who as relator general was theoretically responsible for it, distanced himself from its content. At the press conference at which it was launched, he and Archbishop Bruno Forte, the special secretary of the synod, were both present. When asked about the meaning of the passages relating to homosexuality, Erdo pointed at Forte and remarked, "he who wrote the text must know what it is talking about."[23] The subject of homosexuality particularly divided the synod fathers. In a controversial interview, reported by Edward Pentin, Cardinal Kasper claimed that "Africa is totally different from the West" and that "You can't speak about [homosexuality] with Africans and people of Muslim countries. It's not possible. It's a taboo. For us, we say we ought not to discriminate, we don't want to discriminate in certain respects." He also seemed to suggest that the African bishops' position was only listened to in Africa, "where it's a taboo," but not at the synod. The cardinal continued, "There must be space also for the local bishops' conferences to solve their problems but I'd say with Africa it's impossible [for us to solve]. But they should not tell us too much what we have to do."[24]

Many of the African bishops were angered by Kasper's insinuation that their position was based on a backward "taboo," as well as by his assertion that they should not tell European bishops "too much what we have to do." Kasper initially denied that he had said these words, effectively accusing the journalist in question of lying. It was only when Pentin produced an audio recording of the interview that Kasper issued an apology.

An Objective Half Gained

After the release of the interim report on October 13, the synod fathers separated into small groups to suggest amendments to the text. On the morning of October 16, the reports of the small groups were handed to the synod authorities and it was immediately announced that, contrary to the usual practice, the reports would not be published. This caused immediate uproar in the synod hall as cardinals and bishops rose to their feet, one after the other, to demand publication. It is reported that the synod secretariat was booed and jeered for around fifteen minutes until Pope Francis indicated to Cardinal Baldisseri that the reports could be published.[25]

The importance of their publication was clearly explained by Cardinal Burke:

> I consider the publication of the reports of the ten small groups of critical importance, for they demonstrate that the Synod Fathers do not accept at all the contents of the *Relatio*.... There was an attempt not to publish the reports and to have Father Lombardi

once again filter their contents, but the Synod Fathers, who up to that point were not given any direct means of communication with the public, insisted that the reports be published. It was critical that the public know, through the publication of the reports, that the *Relatio* is a gravely flawed document and does not express adequately the teaching and discipline of the Church and, in some aspects, propagates doctrinal error and a false pastoral approach.[26]

The publication of these reports ensured that the final document had to reflect more accurately the contributions of the synod fathers. In the final version the controversial passages on homosexuality were removed entirely and replaced with short restatements of Catholic teaching. Calls for recognition of the positive aspects of sinful unions remained in the final draft and were accepted by the synod fathers. The passages on the reception of Holy Communion for the divorced and remarried remained in an amended form, but failed to achieve a two-thirds majority. Despite this, Pope Francis ordered that the rejected paragraphs remain in the draft. By acting in this manner, the pope overrode the rules governing the synod. Article 26 § 1 of the *Ordo Synodi Episcoporum* states: "To arrive at the majority of votes, if the vote is for the approval of some item, two thirds of the votes of the Members casting ballots is required; if for the rejection of some item, the absolute majority of the same Members is necessary." By ordering the retention of paragraphs 52, 53, and 55, Pope Francis himself ensured that the "Kasper Proposal" would remain on the agenda of the

Ordinary Synod, despite being rejected by the fathers of the Extraordinary Synod.

The final session of the synod was held on October 18. In his closing speech, Pope Francis delivered a blistering attack on "traditionalists" and "intellectuals." He condemned: "a temptation to hostile inflexibility, that is, wanting to close oneself within the written word, (the letter) and not allowing oneself to be surprised by God, by the God of surprises, (the spirit); within the law, within the certitude of what we know and not of what we still need to learn and to achieve. From the time of Christ, it is the temptation of the zealous, of the scrupulous, of the solicitous, and of the so-called—today—'traditionalists' and also of the intellectuals."

He concluded: "now we still have one year to mature, with true spiritual discernment, the proposed ideas and to find concrete solutions to so many difficulties and innumerable challenges that families must confront."[27]

The implications of this were soon drawn out by Cardinal Marx: "The doors are open—wider than they have ever been since the Second Vatican Council. The synod debates were just a starting point. Francis wants to get things moving, to push processes forward. The real work is about to begin."[28]

The Ordinary Synod

Statements such as this ensured that tension continued to heighten as the 2015 Ordinary Synod approached. One incident, which seemed to represent for many the dubious conduct of the synod process was the story, which broke in February 2015, of the "disappearance" of copies of *Remaining in the Truth of*

Christ that had been sent by Ignatius Press to all synod fathers. According to the account pieced together by Edward Pentin, copies of the book were mailed to each synod father, at the synod hall, in individually addressed envelopes, on the first day of the synod, Monday, October 6. The books were delivered to the Vatican post office on the Thursday or Friday of that week. On arrival they were taken to offices of the synod secretariat. It was here that one of the envelopes is said to have come open, the book identified, and Cardinal Baldisseri informed.

Pentin writes: "According to multiple sources, the cardinal was 'furious' to learn that the book was being sent to the synod fathers...A second source in the secretariat said that a 'discussion' then took place among staff concerning what to do with the books. Cardinal Baldisseri, he said, was 'blowing a gasket' about the book being delivered to the synod."[29]

The same source informed Pentin that Cardinal Baldisseri wanted the delivery of the books blocked but was told by the Vatican's postmaster that that would be illegal. He therefore had the books sent back to the post office in order to be properly stamped as received and then delayed delivery for as long as possible. It was only on the Wednesday of the second week, as the synod was drawing to its close, and nearly a week after they were originally delivered, that the books were finally delivered to the mailboxes of the synod fathers. They were left for a couple of days to fulfill legal requirements and then removed. Most synod fathers therefore never received their copy of this book, which defended the perennial doctrine of the Church.

Disturbing as this incident is, it does not compare to the challenge presented to traditional Catholic doctrine by the publication of the *Instrumentum Laboris,* the working document of the Ordinary Synod, in June 2015. In this document the *Relatio Synodi* of the Extraordinary Synod is supplemented by extensive further commentary, which develops the themes present in the earlier document, as well as addressing some subjects not previously considered. The document contains paragraphs 52, 53, and 55 of the *Relatio Synodi*, despite their rejection by the first synod. However, the problems with the *Instrumentum Laboris* extended far beyond this one issue. Critics argued that the document:

- undermined Church teaching on the intrinsic evil of artificial birth control by proposing a false understanding of the relationship between conscience and the moral law (paragraph 137)
- introduced ambiguity into the Church's teaching on artificial methods of reproduction, such as *in vitro* fertilization, by discussing the "phenomenon" without giving any judgement on the morality of such methods or making any reference to the previous teaching of *Donum vitae* and *Dignitas personae*, or to the loss of human life that results from their use (paragraph 34)[30]
- reduced the indissolubility of marriage to the level of an "ideal" (paragraph 42)
- suggested that cohabitation and "living together" could have "positive aspects" and could, to some extent, be considered legitimate forms of union (paragraphs 57, 61, 63, 99, 102)

- prepared the way for the acceptance of same-sex unions by acknowledging the need to define "the specific character of such unions in society" (paragraph 8)
- denied the full rights of parents regarding the provision of sex education to their children (paragraph 86).

The pro-life coalition, Voice of the Family, concluded that: "The *Instrumentum Laboris*, in common with the *Relatio Post Disceptationem* and *Relatio Synodi* of the Extraordinary Synod, threatens the entire structure of Catholic teaching on marriage, the family and human sexuality."

The composition of the committee that would draft the final report of the synod confirmed such fears. It was clear that at least seven of the ten drafters appointed by Pope Francis were men of known "progressive" views. In addition to Cardinal Baldisseri and Archbishop Bruno Forte, these were: Cardinal Wuerl of Washington, D.C., Cardinal Dew of Wellington, New Zealand,[31] Archbishop Victor Manuel Fernández of Argentina,[32] Bishop Marcello Semeraro of Albano, Italy, and the Jesuit general, Father Adolfo Nicolás.

Pope Francis also made extensive use of his power to make special appointments to the synod to give a voice and a vote to liberal prelates who would not otherwise have been present. Apart from Walter Kasper himself, perhaps his most notorious choice was Cardinal Godfried Danneels, a leading figure in the St. Gallen Group with a record of covering up for a bishop who abused children and of supporting the legalization of abortion

and of homosexual unions. Another controversial papal appoin-
tee was Cardinal Cupich of Chicago, who has openly supported
the admission to the sacraments of unrepentant adulterers and
of practicing homosexuals.

As the opening of the synod became imminent, Cardinal
Robert Sarah voiced the anxieties of many leading churchmen:

> As the starting date for the XIV General Ordinary
> Assembly of the Synod of Bishops dedicated to "The
> Vocation and Mission of the Family in the Church and
> Contemporary World" approaches, the particu-
> lar Churches, the theological faculties, and groups and
> associations of families are intensifying their prepara-
> tions for this major ecclesial event. At the same time,
> there is a sense that opinion makers, pressure groups,
> and lobbies are coming to the fore. We also see com-
> munications strategies being implemented; it would
> even seem that new methodologies for the synod assem-
> bly are being examined in order to give a voice to some
> lines of thought while endeavoring to make others inau-
> dible, if not to silence them completely. Everything leads
> us to believe that the next synod assembly will be for
> many people a synod with high stakes. The future of
> the family is indeed at stake for mankind today.[33]

Sure enough, two days before the synod opened it was
announced that the synod secretariat had "devised a new method"
of conducting the discussions. The synod fathers would spend
much more time in small language-based discussion groups and

comparatively little time in plenary sessions. There would be no *Relatio post disceptationem*, meaning that, unlike the previous year when this interim report revealed the agenda at work and provoked a fight-back, the synod fathers would receive no indication of the content of the final report until the very last day of the synod.

Pope Francis Is Displeased

It was in this context that thirteen cardinals wrote to Pope Francis setting out their key concerns. Among these cardinals were Carlo Caffarra, archbishop of Bologna, Thomas Collins, archbishop of Toronto, Timothy Dolan, archbishop of New York, Willem Eijk, archbishop of Utrecht, Gerhard Ludwig Müller, prefect of the Congregation for the Doctrine of the Faith, Wilfrid Fox Napier, archbishop of Durban, George Pell, prefect of the Secretariat for the Economy, Robert Sarah, prefect of the Congregation for Divine Worship and the Discipline of the Sacraments, Angelo Scola, archbishop of Milan, and Jorge L. Urosa Savino, archbishop of Caracas. The text of the letter, as revealed by Italian journalist Sandro Magister on October 12, 2015, asked Pope Francis to "consider a number of concerns we have heard from other synod fathers, and which we share." Among these concerns were that:

- the *Instrumentum Laboris*, which the "new procedures guiding the synod seem to guarantee…excessive influence," had "various problematic sections," and therefore could not "adequately serve as a guiding text or the foundation of a final document"

- the "new synodal procedures" would "be seen in some quarters as lacking openness and genuine collegiality. In the past, the process of offering propositions and voting on them served the valuable purpose of taking the measure of the synod fathers' minds. The absence of propositions and their related discussions and voting seems to discourage open debate and to confine discussion to small groups; thus it seems urgent to us that the crafting of propositions to be voted on by the entire synod should be restored. Voting on a final document comes too late in the process for a full review and serious adjustment of the text"

- "the lack of input by the synod fathers in the composition of the drafting committee has created considerable unease. Members have been appointed, not elected, without consultation. Likewise, anyone drafting anything at the level of the small circles should be elected, not appointed"

The cardinals concluded: "these things have created a concern that the new procedures are not true to the traditional spirit and purpose of a synod. It is unclear why these procedural changes are necessary. A number of fathers feel the new process seems designed to facilitate predetermined results on important disputed questions."[34]

Reports soon circulated that Pope Francis had fallen into a rage, in the presence of bishops and priests, on receiving the cardinals' letter in Casa Santa Marta. *Il Giornale* mentioned rumors that the pope exclaimed: "If this is the case, they can leave. The

Church does not need them. I will throw them all out!"[35] Other reports had him saying: "Don't they know that I'm the one in charge here? I'll have their red hats."

Whatever the truth of these accounts, the response of Pope Francis in the Synod Hall on October 6 made his position clear. In an unscheduled address to the synod the pope warned against a "hermeneutic of conspiracy" that was "sociologically weak and spiritually unhelpful."[36]

Tilting the Balance

Pope Francis's intervention also dealt with another crisis that had emerged for the "progressive" party, namely, the forthright defense of established Catholic moral teaching by Cardinal Erdo, the general relator of the synod. In his opening report, delivered on the first day of the assembly, Erdo restated the Church's teaching across the whole spectrum of sexual ethics, including decisively rejecting the "Kasper Proposal." Erdo's restatement of Catholic orthodoxy provided encouragement to many synod fathers, but Pope Francis acted decisively to undermine it. In his unscheduled intervention the next morning, Pope Francis instructed the fathers that they should consider the Ordinary Synod to be in perfect continuity with the Extraordinary Synod. He told them that they were to consider only three documents as formal documents of the synod; these were his own opening address at the Extraordinary Synod, the *Relatio* of the Extraordinary Synod, and his own closing address of that synod. He also emphasized that it was the *Instrumentum Laboris* that should guide discussion in the coming days.

This undermined the authority of Cardinal Erdo's report and signaled to the synod fathers that he wished the discussions to proceed along the lines established by the slanted *Relatio Synodi* rather than by Cardinal Erdo. The pope also made it clear that the question of the reception of Holy Communion by the "divorced and remarried" was on the agenda for the synod to consider. The content of the Holy Father's intervention was repeated a number of times by Fr. Lombardi and other speakers at the press conference.[37] Pope Francis's actions seemed to be directed towards weakening Cardinal Erdo's efforts to reorient the Ordinary Synod towards an affirmation and defense of Catholic doctrine.

In many important respects the Ordinary Synod followed a similar course to that of the first assembly. The press office once again seemed to be manipulating the narrative. Fr. Rosica was keen to report an intervention in which it was said that "in the pastoral care of people the language of inclusion must be our language, always considering pastoral and canonical possibilities and solutions." He also made reference to interventions calling for a "new catechesis for marriage," "new language to speak to the people of our time," new "pastoral approaches for those living together before marriage," and a new approach towards homosexuality.

One of the interventions relayed by Rosica was the suggestion that the question of Holy Communion for the divorced and remarried could be solved in different ways in different parts of the world. This would lead to different practices, and implicitly different doctrines, in different parts of the Church. Such calls for "decentralization" were part of the overall strategy adopted by the "progressive" party.[38]

In a major address on October 17, 2015, half-way through the synod, Pope Francis stated that he "felt the need to proceed in a healthy 'decentralization'" of power to the "Episcopal Conferences." "We must reflect on realizing even more through these bodies," he said, because the "hope of the Council that such bodies would help increase the spirit of episcopal collegiality has not yet been fully realized."[39]

The demand for devolution of power, including "genuine doctrinal authority," was repeated by certain synod fathers. Abbot Jeremias Schröder, who attended the synod as a representative of the Union of Superior Generals, said that both "the social acceptance of homosexuality" and the manner of dealing with "divorced and remarried persons" were examples "where bishops' conferences should be allowed to formulate pastoral responses that are in tune with what can be preached and announced and lived in a different context."

The abbot alleged that such delegation was supported by a majority of the synod fathers. "This has come up many times, many interventions in the *aula* have developed the topic that there should be a delegation and authorization of dealing with issues at least pastorally in different ways according to the cultures.... I think I've heard something like that at least twenty times in the interventions, whereas only about two or three have spoken against it, affirming that the unity of the church needs to be maintained also in all these regards and that it would be painful to go into such a delegation of authority."[40]

There was in fact considerable opposition from conservative synod fathers, as was attested by the published interventions of Archbishop Gadecki of Poznan, Archbishop Tomasz

Peta of Kazakhstan, and the major archbishop of Kiev, Sviato-
slav Shevchuk, among others. Yet the resistance of such cardinals
and bishops was unable to prevent the approval of numerous
paragraphs that seemed to undermine, or even directly contradict, previous Catholic teaching.[41] Of particular importance in
this regard was paragraph 85 of the *Relatio* which raised the
question of the "integration" of divorced and remarried Catholics who lack full culpability for their sin. This paragraph is
referenced and built upon in the apostolic exhortation *Amoris
laetitia*. In paragraph 305, and its accompanying footnote (n.
351), Pope Francis indicates that, in certain cases, those living
in an "objective state of sin" may be admitted to the sacraments
of Penance and Holy Communion without amendment of life,
when it is judged that they are not "subjectively culpable" of
mortal sin. This is a departure from established teaching that
those who are objectively guilty of public mortal sin must be
denied admission to the sacraments, despite the existence of factors which might reduce their culpability. With regard to the
divorced and remarried, Pope John Paul II taught: "They are
unable to be admitted thereto from the fact that their state and
condition of life objectively contradict that union of love between
Christ and the Church which is signified and effected by the
Eucharist."[42] There is therefore a clash between the teaching of
paragraph 305 of *Amoris laetitia* and that of paragraph 84 of
Familiaris consortio.

In order to be approved, each paragraph needed, according
to the synod's rules, a two-thirds majority, in this case 177 votes.
Paragraph 85 received 178 votes. If Pope Francis had not added
to the synod, as his own special papal appointments, numerous

individuals—including Cardinal Kasper himself—who were known to support the admission of unrepentant public sinners to the sacraments, the paragraph would not have been approved. This fact alone would validate the assertion that the entirety of the synod was rigged, by the appointments that the pope himself made and the direction he personally imparted to it. Bishop Athanasius Schneider predicted that the manipulation of the synods "will remain for future generations and for historians a black mark which has stained the honor of the Apostolic See."[43]

2. WHAT IS POPE FRANCIS TEACHING? *AMORIS LAETITIA*

Pope Francis followed up the Synod on the Family by publishing in March 2016 the apostolic exhortation *Amoris laetitia*, which was intended to convey the Synod's teaching. At over two hundred pages, the exhortation is difficult to summarize, but its most controversial sections are found mainly in chapter eight. Specifically, paragraph 305, together with its footnote 351, has now been interpreted by various bishops as directly allowing Communion for divorced and civilly remarried Catholics: "Because of forms of conditioning and mitigating factors, it is possible that in an objective situation of sin—which may not be subjectively culpable, or fully such—a person can be living in God's grace, can love and can also grow in the life of grace and charity, while receiving the Church's help to this end." Footnote 351 followed this saying plainly, "In certain cases this can include the help of the sacraments."

Although controversy raged over the correct, or intended, interpretation of these passages, with many bishops insisting that it is impossible for a papal document to contradict previous teaching, the bishops of Buenos Aires issued their guidelines in September 2016.[44] They conceded that "priests may suggest a decision to live in continence," but said that "if the partners fail in this purpose," after following "a discernment process," *Amoris laetitia* "offers the possibility of having access to the Sacrament of Reconciliation," without an intention to cease engaging in marital relations.[45]

While the interpretation controversy continued, Francis maintained silence and has not corrected bishops like Charles Chaput of Philadelphia and Stanisław Gadecki of Poznan, who have taken the conservative position. But the only endorsements from the pope have been sent to the bishops of Buenos Aires and Malta[46] in the form of letters thanking them for their liberal interpretations. Francis wrote to his former Argentinian colleagues thanking them for their "very good" guidelines that "fully capture the meaning of chapter VIII of 'Amoris Laetitia.'" To drive home the point, the pope added, "There are no other interpretations."[47] A similar letter was reportedly sent to Malta through the Pope's proxy, the secretary general of the Synods of Bishops, Cardinal Lorenzo Baldisseri.

In view of the differing interpretations, and the apparent subjectivity which *Amoris laetitia* introduced into Catholic moral teaching, a number of cardinals addressed to the pope a letter requesting clarification of the document. The signatories are now known to number six, although only four names have been made public—Cardinals Brandmüller, Burke, Caffarra,

and Meisner—but they are said to have the support of some
twenty or thirty others. They began by sending to the pope and
to the prefect of the Congregation for the Doctrine of the Faith
a private letter on September 19, 2016, with the requests mentioned. These were couched in the traditional form of *dubia*,
(disputed points that are submitted to the Congregation for the
Doctrine of the Faith when the Church's teaching appears to
be uncertain). The five *dubia* may be summarized as follows:

1. Has it become licit to admit the divorced and
   remarried to Holy Communion?
2. Is it still Catholic teaching that there exist absolute
   moral norms?
3. Are those who are living in violation of a commandment, such as the commandment against
   adultery, to be considered as living in objective sin?
4. Is it still Catholic teaching that circumstances or
   intentions can never transform an act intrinsically
   evil into an act "subjectively" good?
5. Is it still Catholic teaching that conscience cannot
   legitimate exceptions to absolute moral norms?

To these queries the Congregation for the Doctrine of the
Faith refused to reply, in contrast to normal practice, and it is
clear that it was acting on Pope Francis's orders. In view of this,
the signatories made their letter public in November, thus bringing their challenge to the teaching of *Amoris laetitia* into the
open.[48] The pope made no explicit reply, but he is reported to
have encouraged those around him to discredit the dissidents by

indirect means, and spokesmen for the "progressive" wing of the Church have expressed shocked indignation that anyone could misunderstand the pope's emphasis on the new "openness" of Catholic teaching.[49] What this openness is precisely, the Church has not yet discovered, since Francis does not answer the questions put to him. To deduce where the pope is intending to take the Church's teaching, we need to study the policy he has followed in the Vatican's bodies designed to guard the institution of the family.

The Overhaul of the Pontifical Academy for Life

From 1978 to the reign of Benedict XVI, those involved in defending traditional Catholic ethics became accustomed to looking to the Vatican as a bulwark of support for their cause, particularly in the fight against abortion. The combination of John Paul II, the "pro-life pope," and Cardinal Ratzinger backing him up in the Congregation for the Doctrine of the Faith gave the Vatican the last word on a host of moral questions of critical importance in politics. This moral authority was respected even by non-Catholic conservatives who followed the Vatican's lead on complex issues like new reproductive technologies, cloning, and stem-cell research. Although the Congregation for the Doctrine of the Faith played a crucial role in developing the pro-life position, one of the main organs of Catholic thought on these issues was the body established in 1994, the Pontifical Academy for Life, dedicated to studying "the principal problems of biomedicine and of law, relative to the promotion and defense of life, above all in the direct relation that they have with Christian morality and the directives of the Church's Magisterium."

Founded by John Paul II and the renowned pro-life doctor and geneticist Jérôme Lejeune,[50] the *Pontificia Academia Pro Vita* boasted some of the most serious Catholic minds in Europe, including the philosophers Michel Schooyans and Josef Seifert and the bio-ethicist Elio Sgreccia. Not all members were as well known, but all life members were required to take the "oath of the Servants of Life," which bound them to uphold Catholic teaching on the sanctity of human life in all its stages.

Even before the resignation of Pope Benedict, cracks started to show in the *Pontificia Academia Pro Vita*. Signs of a change began in 2008 with the appointment as president of Archbishop Rino Fisichella, an upwardly mobile career Vatican official with a less than complete attachment to Catholic teaching on life issues. In 2009, Fisichella criticized a Brazilian bishop for publicly confirming the excommunication of doctors who had procured an abortion of twin babies carried by a nine-year-old victim of rape. According to Church law, abortion is among the *"graviora delicta,"* offences so serious that they incur excommunication automatically, without the need for an official declaration. Fisichella wrote, however, that the doctors had been justified because, he claimed, they had acted to save the girl's life.

Bishop Cardoso Sobrinho of Recife later clarified that the child and her family had been under the care of doctors who were prepared to save the lives of the twins by caesarean section with no harm to the girl.[51] He was forced to make a public declaration of the excommunications, because of false reports that the young mother had been excommunicated, which was not the case, as she was "not morally responsible for this tragic act." Bishop Sobrinho added: "My hope is that those affected by the excommunication they brought upon themselves may change their hearts and may not wait until the proximity of death to repent." The incident was a cause célèbre in Brazil and the bishop had been fighting a running battle with the secular press and abortion campaigners. Fisichella's statement that the doctors did not merit excommunication, which appeared in an article in the Vatican's newspaper *L'Osservatore Romano*, was taken, therefore, as a sign that the Vatican was siding in the affair against its own bishop and teaching, and as Fisichella doubled down, attacking his critics, this impression was strengthened.

The article caused an instant uproar in the secular press, with liberal reporters and columnists hailing it as a signal that the Catholic Church would soon modify its intransigent position on abortion. Five members of *Pontificia Academia Pro Vita* responded in public against the article, but, as is often the way in the modern Vatican, Fisichella's career was boosted by the scandal.[52] After two years of disputes between the pro-life members and Fisichella, he was removed in 2010, but was placed in his current position as head of the Pontifical Council for the New Evangelization—a posting that involves a high public profile and close association with the pope, and thus seems like a papal reward.

In the years following, the *Pontificia Academia Pro Vita* continued to generate concerns for pro-life advocates on a variety of topics, including its endorsement of explicit sex education for children, developed by the Pontifical Council for the Family and released during World Youth Day in Poland. In 2012 Josef Seifert wrote an open letter to Fisichella's replacement, Monsignor Ignacio Carrasco de Paula, warning that the *Pontificia Academia Pro Vita* was in danger of betraying its founding purpose after the organization's 18th General Assembly appeared to endorse *in vitro* fertilization, a process condemned by the Congregation for the Doctrine of the Faith's documents *Donum vitae* (1987) and *Dignitas personae* (2008).

The American doyenne of pro-life activists, Judie Brown of the American Life League, was another of the original corresponding members of the *Pontificia Academia Pro Vita* who had opposed Fisichella's endorsement of abortion. She commented in February 2017 that Pope Francis has "deconstructed" the *Pontificia Academia Pro Vita* with his new statutes and membership appointments, saying it is "one of the most heartbreaking events I have seen in my lifetime. But given the politics of the Vatican, it is not surprising." She wondered whether Archbishop Fisichella's denial that abortion merited automatic excommunication was "the beginning of the end" for the *Pontificia Academia Pro Vita*. "Several subsequent occurrences, including by the current Academy president, Archbishop Vincenzo Paglia, in support of the Vatican's version of sex education, do not bode well for the Academy and its future," Brown said.

Pope Francis gave pro-family, pro-life advocates, and supporters of traditional Catholic teaching reason to worry from the beginning of his pontificate. In July 2013, he made his now-famous "Who am I to judge?" comment about the notorious Fr. Battista Ricca, the homosexual priest who was his "eyes and ears" monitoring financial reform in the Vatican.[53] The *New York Times* called the comment—made while the pope was talking with reporters on a plane back to Rome from World Youth Day in Rio de Janeiro—"revolutionary," and noted that in the course of his comments, Francis became the first pope to use the colloquial term "gay" to describe a homosexual. The *New York Times* observed: "Francis's words could not have been more different from those of Benedict XVI, who in 2005 wrote that…men with 'deep-seated homosexual tendencies' should not become priests." In thanks for his comment, Pope Francis was immediately elevated to the status of hero of the homosexual political lobby (even though, ironically, in his extended comments, he had, with the ambiguity that characterized many of his early statements, actually said, "one must distinguish the fact of being a gay person from the fact of doing a lobby, because not all lobbies are good. That's bad…. The problem isn't having this tendency, no…. The problem is the lobbying of this tendency,") and the homosexual activist magazine *Advocate* featured his face on its cover and declared him "person of the year."

The following September, he forced pro-life advocates into damage control when he said the Catholic world should not "obsess" over abortion, "gay marriage," and contraception. In a lengthy interview with Antonio Spadaro in *La Civiltà Cattolica*, Francis said, "It is not necessary to talk about these issues all the time. The dogmatic and moral teachings of the church are not all equivalent. The church's pastoral ministry cannot be obsessed with the transmission of a disjointed multitude of doctrines to be imposed insistently."

In October 2016, a year after the second Synod on the Family and in the midst of the developing furor over the *dubia*, Pope Francis redirected the *Pontificia Academia Pro Vita* on a new trajectory, approving new statutes, dismissing all of its members, and instituting five-year terms for everyone. The new rules also abolished the Lejeune oath of fidelity to Catholic teaching and allowed non-Catholics to be appointed.[54]

Christine Vollmer, the Venezuelan founder of a refuge for women and a founding member whom Francis removed from her life membership, commented on the change: "Originally we each had to make an oath in front of the Nuncio of our country that we would be Servants of Life and uphold the teaching on life of the Magisterium. We have not seen of course the new 'commitment' but the wording on the new statutes sounds softer, and as the Academy is now open to people of any religion or none, it is doubtful they would commit very seriously to *Humanae Vitae*!"[55]

Vollmer warned that since the death of Dr. Lejeune the *Pontificia Academia Pro Vita* has become "ever more directed towards 'hard science' rather than 'pro-life science.'" The academy, she said, "was founded with a list of intentionally mixed specialists including lawyers, doctors, journalists, pro-life leaders, psychiatrists, family activists, priests, teachers, and so on, the intention of the founders being to be able to study and analyse the causes of anti-life tendencies and find ways to counteract them."

Indeed, the new statutes included language not previously seen from any Vatican dicastery. The academy's defense of life must, it said, include "the promotion of a quality of human life that integrates its material and spiritual value with a view to an authentic 'human ecology' that helps recover the original balance of creation between the human person and the entire universe."

The author, however, did not offer any definitions that would explain this rather grandiose requirement.

Francis followed this in June 2017 by appointing forty-five new full members, of whom only thirteen were re-appointments. Perhaps the most notable of the non-Catholics is Japanese Nobel laureate in medicine Shinya Yamanaka, the developer of a controversial method of cloning "embryo-like" stem cells. Another of Francis's ecumenical choices is the Anglican Nigel Biggar. His appointment caused outrage when the *Catholic Herald*[56] revealed that he had told the philosopher Peter Singer that an eighteen-week gestational limit is acceptable for legal abortion because the fetus does not have the same moral status as an adult human being. The *Herald* quoted Biggar saying, "It's not clear that a human foetus is the same kind of thing as an adult or a mature human being, and therefore deserves quite the same treatment. It then becomes a question of where we draw the line, and there is no absolutely cogent reason for drawing it in one place over another."

In light of this, Biggar's mild opposition to legalized euthanasia—on the grounds it would create "a radically libertarian society at the cost of a socially humane one,"—seems a weak qualification for membership in a pontifical academy originally dedicated to the Church's teaching on the sanctity of human life.

Thirteen members were confirmed from the previous roster, but they notably did not include academic luminaries and long-standing defenders of Catholic moral teaching who had been with the academy from the beginning and been close to Pope John Paul II and Benedict. Among those dropped from the academy were the Belgian philosopher Michel Schooyans, Austria's Josef

Seifert, the German Robert Spaemann, and the Englishman Luke Gormally, all of whom had been vocal critics of the two family synods, *Amoris laetitia*, and Archbishop Fisichella. Also dropped were the Australian philosopher John Finnis and the renowned American-French bio-ethicist Germain Grisez who coauthored an "open letter" to Pope Francis highly critical of *Amoris laetitia*. Others cut were a group of central European psychologists who were notable opponents of "gender ideology," Andrzej Szostek (Poland), Mieczyslaw Grzegocki (Ukraine), and Jaroslav Sturma (Czech Republic). Francis's treatment of the *Pontificia Academia Pro Vita* seemed to imply that not only would he demand absolute loyalty from prelates but he would purge troublesome laymen who opposed his plans.

Indeed, among the most prominent omissions from those invited to participate in the 2014 Synod on the Family was any representative of the John Paul II Institute for Studies on Marriage and Family. The institute was founded by Pope John Paul II in 1982 following the 1980 Synod on the Family and the promulgation of his apostolic exhortation *Familiaris consortio,* and has been steadily growing, to ten affiliates around the world. It was this document of John Paul II, which reasserted the impossibility for the civilly remarried of receiving Communion, that was to come under attack at the synods of Pope Francis.

The John Paul II Institute issued a series of papers in the buildup to the 2014 synod, reiterating classical Catholic moral teaching as articulated in *Familiaris consortio*, and plainly aimed at the Kasper Proposal. One of their papers, "The Gospel of the Family: Going Beyond Cardinal Kasper's Proposal in the Debate on Marriage, Civil Re-Marriage and Communion in the Church," had a foreword by Cardinal Pell and was published simultaneously in Italy, the United States, Spain, and Germany. At a preliminary conference in Rome in early October 2014, the philosophy professor Stanislaw Grygiel, who had been close to Karol Wojtyla and taught at the institute, gave a hint as to why the institute had been excluded from the synods. He directly refuted the premise of the Kasper Proposal:

> A "merciful" indulgence, requested by some theologians, is not capable of stopping the advancement of the hardness of hearts that do not remember how things are "from the beginning." The Marxist assumption according to which philosophy must change the world rather than contemplating it has made inroads into the thinking of certain theologians such that these, more or less deliberately, instead of looking at man and the world in the light of the eternal Word of the living God, look at this Word from the perspective of ephemeral sociological tendencies. As a result they justify the actions of 'hard hearts" according to the circumstances, and speak of the mercy of God as if this were a matter of tolerance tinged with commiseration.
>
> A theology constituted in this way demonstrates a disregard for man. For these theologians man is no longer mature enough to look with courage, in the light of divine mercy, at the truth of his own becoming love, just as this truth itself is "from the beginning" (Mt 19:8).

Following the synods, in September 2016, Pope Francis disregarded the institute's rules, which stipulate that its chancellor must be the vicar general of Rome, by appointing Archbishop Paglia in that role, and as the new president Msgr. Pierangelo Sequeri, an apparent ally who supported Francis in the controversy over *Amoris laetitia*. Soon after this, the pope canceled an opening-of-term address by Cardinal Robert Sarah and gave the address himself, in which he rebuked theologians who offer "a far too abstract and almost artificial theological ideal of marriage." Edward Pentin wrote of Paglia's and Sequeri's appointments that "given their backgrounds, and at a time when St. John Paul II's teaching in this area appears to be judged inappropriate, their arrival as heads of the pontifical institute is undoubtedly a cause for concern among those who work there and further afield."

The future of the institute's devotion to *Familiaris consortio* remains in doubt. In October 2016, Archbishop Denis Hart announced the closure of the Melbourne branch of the institute, alleging that it had attracted too few students to justify the financial outlay. But Dan Hitchens, deputy editor of the *Catholic Herald*, linked the closure to the opposition of the institute to the direction taken by the synods and noted that not only had student enrollment been growing, but that Melbourne is "one of the wealthiest dioceses in the world" with the resources to buy a large building in 2011 for A$36 million, "enough money to keep the JPII Institute going for decades."

Hitchens wrote, "There is an elephant in the room: the John Paul II Institute has many enemies in Australia.... The institute's supporters viewed it as 'a shining light of Catholic orthodoxy

amidst a swamp of modernism in so much of the Catholic edu-
cational structure.' That attachment to orthodoxy made it
unpopular."

Archbishop Vincenzo Paglia

Not well known outside Italy, Vincenzo Paglia has been a
leading figure on the Italian Church's Left for decades. While he
has occasionally spoken in support of traditional Catholic moral
teaching, his habitual ambiguity makes him an echo of Pope
Francis. In August 2015, under his leadership, the Pontifical
Council for the Family[57] issued a book that proposed arguments
for allowing divorced and civilly remarried Catholics to receive
Communion after following a "discretionary path," essentially
a reiteration of Cardinal Kasper's proposal. On this, perhaps the
most vexed subject in the contemporary Church, Paglia himself
has maintained in public a studied ambiguity. He called it "phar-
isaical to limit ourselves to repeating laws and denouncing sins."
The Church, he said, "must be ready to find new paths to follow."

In February 2017 Archbishop Paglia aroused a storm of
protest when he eulogized Marco Pannella, the founder of Italy's
Radical Party, calling him "a man of great spirituality." He said
that Pannella—whose party had pressed for the legalization of
divorce, contraception, abortion, and euthanasia, as well as
drugs—had "spent his life for the least" in "defence of the dignity
of all, especially the most marginalized." Paglia called Pannella's
life an "inspiration for a more beautiful life not only for Italy, but
for our world, which needs more than ever men who can talk like
him.... I hope that the spirit of Marco can help us to live in that

same direction." The speech prompted calls for Paglia's resignation as head of the Pontifical Academy for Life and the John Paul II Institute for Studies on Marriage and the Family.

Paglia had been making headlines since at least 2012 as a clerical supporter of the homosexual political movement, always maintaining enough ambiguity to ensure deniability. In February 2013, just weeks before Pope Benedict's resignation, he told an interviewer that the state ought to grant legal recognition to "de facto" or cohabiting couples, including homosexuals. This was at the time the Italian parliament was debating a law granting homosexual partners legal rights similar to natural marriage.

Paglia's appointment was further evidence that the *Pontificia Academia Pro Vita* was being redirected from its founding purpose. The appointment of Nigel Biggar is thought to have been suggested by Paglia, and given Biggar's support for legalized abortion and his denial of the personhood of the unborn child from the moment of conception, it raises the question of how seriously either Pope Francis or Archbishop Paglia intend to take their own statutes.[58]

As for his work as head of the Pontifical Academy for Life, the case of the seriously ill British child, Charlie Gard,[59] gave further insight into Archbishop Paglia's view of life issues. Charlie Gard's parents had been waging a court and media battle asserting their rights to determine their son's treatment, against doctors who had determined that the child should be "allowed to die" and refused to release him from hospital. Paglia issued a statement that in essence gave preference to the right of the state (in a system of socialized medicine) over the right of the parents to determine the boy's treatment, saying that the parents should "not be left to face their painful decisions alone." Michael Brendan Dougherty riposted in *National Review*:

> Besides being patronizing, the Vatican's statement is a gross distortion of the situation. It portrays the Gards as acting alongside the doctors, but subject to outside manipulation. The Gards are resisting the doctors. The Gards are not facing "their decisions." They are facing authorities that have overridden them. The good bishop writes that the Gards "must be heard and respected, but they too must be helped to understand the unique difficulty of their situation." The people "helping" them to understand are speaking in the euphemisms of "death with dignity."[60]

So great was the uproar against Paglia's statement that the pope intervened, perhaps anticipating a media disaster if the Church were seen opposing both its own teaching and the desires of the grief-stricken parents. Damage control came in the form of a note posted to the pope's Twitter account two days after Paglia's statement, saying, "To defend human life, above all when it is wounded by illness, is a duty of love that God entrusts to all."[61]

A further sidelight on Archbishop Paglia's career is that while he was Bishop of Terni he had commissioned for his cathedral a mural by the Argentinian homosexual painter Ricardo Cinalli. The mural depicts an almost nude Christ figure (whose face was based on that of a male hairdresser) lifting two nets filled with naked or semi-naked sinners being taken to heaven, including a nude depiction of Paglia himself. Cinalli confirmed that Paglia had approved every stage of the work; he added that Paglia had drawn the line only at depicting the figures in the act of copulating, but added "that the erotic aspect is the most notable among the people inside the nets." This was the churchman Francis chose to be head of the John Paul II Institute for Studies on Marriage and the Family and the Pontifical Academy for Life.

What Does It All Mean?

We are left with the question of what Pope Francis intends to teach in the field of the family and sexual morality. One piece of evidence is a conversation related by Archbishop Bruno Forte, whom Francis appointed as special secretary for the synods. At a conference on *Amoris laetitia* in May 2016, Forte said that before the synods the pope had told him, "If we speak explicitly about Communion for the divorced and remarried, you don't know what a terrible mess we will make. So we won't speak plainly, do it in a way that the premises are there, then I will draw out the conclusions." On this Archbishop Forte joked: "Typical of a Jesuit."[62] Perhaps so. Those who know the Society of Jesus might reply that it is not the way the great Jesuit theologians such as St. Robert Bellarmine taught in days gone by, though it may be the impression that some supple members of the order have given in times of decline. If that is the strand of the Jesuit tradition that Francis has brought to the papal throne, the Church has reaped an unfortunate harvest.

In his five-year reign, Pope Francis has not been backward with adjurations and rebukes, and his trademark has been to attack pharisaism and insincerity and call us back to the true spirit of Christ's teaching. But one precept he seems to have overlooked is, "Let your yea be yea and your nay be nay." Amid the sound bites and the ambiguities, the faithful are left wondering what he intends to teach. Conservatives are appalled at the abandonment of positions for which John Paul II and Benedict XVI stood firm; liberals are no happier with the vague teaching of *Amoris laetitia*. That document does not make clear whether the Church really intends to admit the divorced and remarried to Communion, and it leaves untouched the other questions of sexual morality, from abortion to homosexuality, which they hoped to see addressed. In some respects Pope Francis has shown himself an enemy óf liberalism; he has repeatedly condemned abortion (though not without confusing signals) and he has spoken strongly against "gender ideology." But if his liberalizing program is the true way ahead, could we not expect him to preach it with the clarity and courage of one who speaks in the spirit of Christ?

A range of serious, unanswered questions are posed by Francis's pontificate. Can we be sure that Catholic teaching still condemns abortion, or is that teaching being modified by the Protestants and agnostics who have been brought into the Pontifical Academy for Life? Francis tells us that the Church in the past upheld an "artificial ideal of marriage," but what is the doctrine of marriage that he is now preaching to us? What does it mean that, under Pope Francis, the Congregation for the Doctrine of the Faith will not answer whether Catholic teaching believes in objective moral norms, and that it seems to be thought an offence to ask the question? How is it that a man like Archbishop Paglia is judged fit to head the John Paul II Institute for Studies on Marriage and the Family and the Pontifical Academy for Life? Can we expect, under his patronage, to find homo-erotic murals sprouting on the walls of Catholic churches from San Francisco to Manila? If so, will Pope Francis shrug it off with, "Who am I to judge?" Or will he tell us anything at all? On a more general level, does Francis believe that his flock deserve the answers to such questions, or are they just brainless sheep, to be driven wherever their master chooses to push them?

Chapter 5

MERCY! MERCY!

"The Church is a love story. If we do not understand this we have understood nothing of what the Church is."

—**POPE FRANCIS**, morning meditation in the chapel of the Casa Santa Marta, April 24, 2013

1. THE DESTRUCTION OF THE FRANCISCAN FRIARS OF THE IMMACULATE

When Jorge Mario Bergoglio stepped out on the *loggia* of St Peter's Basilica and became the first pope to assume the name Francis, he seemed to be a perfect fit as the reform pope the public had wanted. By using that name he chose to pay homage to the great medieval saint and reformer St. Francis of Assisi, who is now most closely associated with "holy poverty," the main theme of the new pope's pontificate. Selective hagiography has reduced St. Francis to a sandal-wearing, animal-loving pacifist, but the real man was a stern defender of the faith, preaching obedience to God through His Church. Far from having an aversion to active proselytism— forthrightly calling non-Catholics to convert—St. Francis, a

137

former soldier, traveled to Egypt to confront the sultan and preach the name of Christ at the risk of martyrdom. At the same time his letters attest to his insistence on honoring God in the liturgy with precious and beautiful altar furnishings.

Authentic "Franciscan" spirituality was rediscovered and reembodied in our own times with the founding of a new religious institute, the Franciscan Friars of the Immaculate, in 1970 in Frigento, Italy. Fathers Stefano Maria Manelli and Gabriel Maria Pellettieri were Conventual Franciscans who wanted to return to a more rigorous form of religious life. Manelli is considered a pioneer in the spiritual life, having authored the *Traccia Mariana*, a Marian plan for Franciscan life expounding the order's charism, prayer, and dedication to the Virgin Mary. It can be seen as the core of the institute's unique spirituality.

The new institute's special dedication to Mary was rooted in the spirituality of St. Maximilian Kolbe, the Polish Franciscan who died in Auschwitz. In 1990, the institute was raised to the status of an "institute of diocesan right" by the archbishop of Benevento. While the rest of the Church fell into a serious vocations crisis, vocations to the Franciscan Friars of the Immaculate abounded and soon the need for a women's branch became evident. In 1993 the bishop of Monte Cassino erected the Franciscan Sisters of the Immaculate, a religious institute of women who lived according to the *Regula Bullata*[1] and the *Traccia*.

In 1998, Pope John Paul II made the Franciscans Friars of the Immaculate an "institute of religious life of pontifical right," and extended this recognition to the sister branch the same year. The institute continued to grow, spreading throughout the world to Argentina, Australia, Austria, Benin, Brazil, Cameroon, Chad,

France, Italy, Portugal, Nigeria, the Philippines, and the United States. It served especially in poor countries where it was difficult to find other orders to take up missionary work. Father Manelli followed the ideal set out by the Vatican II decree, *Perfectae caritatis*, on the renewal of the religious life that called for a "return to the sources," the original charisms of the founders of the religious orders.

From their history and their spirit, the Franciscans of the Immaculate seemed to be all that St. Francis stood for and every-thing that Pope Francis could want from a religious institute: strictest poverty, an intense prayer life, and a missionary com-mitment. Poverty especially was lived by the Friars in a literal fashion: their communities lived off donations, waiting for Prov-idence to find people willing to provide for them. One might call it a case study in Pope Francis's insistence on poverty and helping the poor.

Yet only a few months after Pope Francis's appearance on St. Peter's *loggia*, the history of the Friars would take a turn for the worse. The story of what can only be described as the papal persecution of a flourishing religious order will perhaps be remembered as one of the strangest of the modern era.

One Fatal Error: Love of Liturgical Tradition

In the last years of the pontificate of Benedict XVI, the Friars of the Immaculate had begun to use the pre-Vatican II order of the Mass. Even after the issue of Benedict's *motu proprio, Summorum pontificum*, in 2007, the use of the older liturgical form has been broadly opposed by bishops, especially in Italy. Nevertheless, interest in its use has seen a steady growth, and it may have been this growing interest in the traditional forms of liturgy among the Friars of the Immaculate's younger vocations that drew the ire of the Vatican. When the order voted to use the Old Rite preferentially they immediately became the second largest group in the Church to do so, with more than two hundred priests, 360 brothers, and four hundred nuns. The signal to the broader Church of this popular community abandoning the Ordinary Form could not be endured by men dedicated to the new Catholic paradigm.

The Friars of the Immaculate began the regular use of the Old Rite after the publication of *Summorum pontificum*. At the 2008 general chapter they took the decision to adopt the Extraordinary Form of the Mass throughout the order, while continuing to celebrate the Ordinary Form in communities and parishes entrusted to them; this attempt to go "bi-ritual" was to be catastrophic. Sensitive to the political ramifications of being labeled "traditionalists," Father Manelli made it a point to continue to celebrate the Ordinary Form when he made visitations to the order's parishes. He was at pains to explain that his friars were not rejecting Vatican II in their liturgical decision. In May 2012, the general chapter of the Franciscan Sisters of the Immaculate, as well as the contemplative branch, also expressed a preference for the use of the Old Rite in their chapels.

Until late in 2011 this decision received little notice from Rome. In a letter written by Father Manelli and his advisors dated November 21, 2011, the general secretary of the Friars sent some indicative norms for the use of the Extraordinary Form to all houses, with some communities giving priority to the Old Rite and others keeping the Ordinary Form. These were approved by the Pontifical Commission *Ecclesia Dei* in a letter of April 14, 2012.

The Decree and the Start of
Open Persecution

This changed when the Brazilian Cardinal João Braz de Aviz was appointed to the Congregation for Religious in January 2011: the following year he ordered an investigation into the order's affairs. On July 11, 2013, the Congregation issued a decree demanding that every priest of the Friars of the Immaculate cease using the Old Rite of the Mass. "If the occasion should arise, the use of the extraordinary form (Vetus Ordo) must be explicitly authorized by the competent authorities, for every religious and/or community that makes the request." The Congregation for Religious dissolved the order's General Council and appointed an apostolic commissioner, the Capuchin Father Fidenzio Volpi, as effective superior of all the communities of the congregation and whose expenses it was told to pay. It also became widely known that there were mysterious "allegations" against the order and its founder, Father Manelli, but both Volpi and the Vatican refused to clarify these, while rumors flew around the internet. They included sinister tales of an unspecified "secret vow"[2] that members were ordered to take. Lurid stories were leaked to the tabloid press, with anonymous "former sisters" claiming that the sisters were ordered to write their vows in blood and "flagellate" themselves for the length of "five Our Fathers, five Ave Marias, and five Salve Reginas."[3]

Slowly, however, the realities became clear as information was filtered out by more credible sources, often later to be corroborated by officials. It became known that a group of five or six "dissidents" in the order had complained to Cardinal Braz de Aviz, particularly objecting to the use of the Old Rite but hinting darkly at other, soon-to-be-announced misdemeanors that in the end never emerged.

Among these dissidents was Father Alfonso Maria Bruno, who was well known for media work that made him popular in Italy. Father Bruno was quickly appointed spokesman of the order in Italy, and told the Catholic News Agency that the issue of the Mass was "only the tip of the iceberg," though he declined to specify what lay beneath that tip. The Friars of the Immaculate were now widely suspected of some kind of improper behavior, a "kiss of death" innuendo given the alarm over the priestly sexual abuse scandals. Another major name in the saga is that of the American Father Angelo M. Geiger. He too had an extensive social media presence and was to become the order's effective internet gatekeeper, filtering information through the order's YouTube and Facebook accounts and website. Father Bruno went so far as to accuse the congregation's contemplative sisters of possibly falling into "heresy and disobedience." Since no journalist was allowed access to anyone but Father Bruno and Father Geiger, it was impossible to verify such claims.

With all this innuendo, the Friars and Sisters of the Immaculate felt it necessary to release an "official" note on August 3, 2013, explaining that the allegations were untrue. Father Manelli "not only has never imposed on all the…communities the use— much less the exclusive use—of the *Vetus Ordo*, but he does not even want it to become the exclusive use, and he has personally given the example, celebrating everywhere according to the one and the other *Ordo*." This response had little effect, however; the decree of the Vatican, putting the Friars of the Immaculate under the supervision of Father Volpi, was carried out, and greatly exceeded, over the next three years.

The treatment of the Friars of the Immaculate was indicative of Pope Francis's way of handling those he considered dissidents from his progressive program. Church law includes principles of evidence and due process, but no specific, proven cause of misconduct was ever stated in the decree regarding the Mass and the governing structure of the Friars of the Immaculate. The reasons for the canonical measures taken seemed insufficient, even trivial.

The second signatory to the decree, Archbishop José Rodríguez Carballo, is a figure of special importance. The Vaticanist Sandro Magister wrote: "Rodríguez Carballo...enjoys the pope's complete trust. His promotion as second-in-command of the congregation [the Congregation for Religious] was backed by Francis himself at the beginning of his pontificate." Rodríguez Carballo's appointment to the Congregation for Religious was in fact the pope's first major Vatican appointment in April 2013, less than a month after the Conclave. But Rodríguez Carballo already had a notorious reputation, having previously been involved in a large financial scandal during his ten years as general minister of the Franciscan Order, before his appointment to the Vatican. The scandal had put the financial stability of the Franciscan order into danger, as Father Michael Perry, Carballo's successor, disclosed in a letter to his brothers. What the media called a "maxi-fraud" had hit the order of the Franciscans hard: fraud and embezzlement of tens of millions of euros brought it to its financial knees. Under the rule of Rodríguez Carballo, the order had invested money in offshore companies in Switzerland which had in turn been involved in arms-dealing, drug-trafficking, and money-laundering.

It appears that he allowed the intentional mismanagement of funds in Italy by persons outside the order, who enriched themselves with help from members of the order. Father Michael Perry wrote in his letter that the order "finds itself in grave, and I underscore 'grave', financial difficulty, with a significant burden of debt," and added, "The systems of financial oversight and control for the management of the patrimony of the Order were either too weak or were compromised, thus limiting their effectiveness to guarantee responsible, transparent management." Friars had been involved in "a number of questionable financial activities" and Father Perry had to call in lawyers and civil authorities to investigate the scandal.

Without waiting for the full report of the Swiss authorities on the case of the Franciscans, Pope Francis promoted Archbishop José Rodríguez Carballo to a more influential and higher-ranking position in the Church hierarchy because he considered him a trustworthy ally.

Father Fidenzio Volpi's "Reign of Terror"

Father Manelli's reaction to the July decree that put new restriction on the Friars of the Immaculate has been held up as exemplary. Despite being in the line of fire and subsequently blamed for mismanaging the institute and worse crimes, the order's founder commended the whole institute to obedience to the Holy Father and expressed his trust that this obedience would bring forth "greater graces." His hope might have been that the new pope would foster an objective evaluation of the situation of the institute and bring justice in a situation where a handful of friars had rebelled against the majority of their institute.

It was revealed that Father Volpi—who maintained that his "work" had been "specifically ordered by the Vicar of Christ"—had been instructed to subdue "dissent" in the ranks, establish unity, and assess the order's finances. In effect, it was a complete take-over of the institute—priests, friars, sisters, and tertiaries. Father Volpi's rule was ruthless: the general government was deposed and the founder Father Manelli was placed under *de facto* house arrest, being ordered to remain in seclusion in the south of Italy. A petition was written against the ban of the Extraordinary Form by four lay scholars but was ignored.

Already by December 2013 many Catholics had had enough and circulated a petition asking for the removal of Father Volpi. "In the space of five months, Fr. Volpi has destroyed the institute, provoking chaos and suffering within, scandal amongst the faithful, criticism from the press, uneasiness and perplexity in the ecclesiastical world." This letter too was ignored.

On December 8, 2013, Father Volpi responded with another series of sanctions, including the closure of the order's seminary, in a letter addressed to all the Friars. In it he lamented the "disobedience and obstacles set in the way of my work, as well as attitudes of suspicion and criticism towards our holy mother the Church—even to the point of slanderously accusing her of the 'destruction of the charism' through my person."

This letter makes the first "official" charge of misconduct against Father Manelli who, he said, had "transferred control" of assets of the institute to members of the laity, "persons known to be spiritual children or relatives of the Founder, Fr. Stefano M. Manelli, as well as to the parents of various sisters," to save them from the Commissioner's influence. Father Volpi denounced those religious who wanted to petition for the foundation of a new institute focused on the Old Rite. He also ordered the lay organization of tertiaries to be suspended until further notice.

With seminary studies interrupted and the institute's private study program suspended, theology students were moved to Rome to continue their work. Philosophy students were sent to the diocesan college of Benevento. Diaconal and priestly ordinations were suspended for one year. All candidates for Holy Orders were asked to formally subscribe to their acceptance of the Ordinary Form of the Mass and the "documents of the Second Vatican Council" in what was being referred to as an "oath" of compliance. Candidates who would not comply were immediately dismissed from the institute. Furthermore, every religious had to express in written form his willingness to continue as a Franciscan Friar of the Immaculate in the institute's revised form. The lay Mission of the Immaculate Mediatrix in Italy was formally suspended, as well as the Third Order of the Franciscan Friars of the Immaculate and all publishing activities—a major work of the order—were halted.

Fr. Volpi promoted one of the original five dissidents, Father Bruno, to general secretary. (He has since been removed.) Under Father Manelli, Bruno had been in charge of public relations including social media networks. His position in relation to the media was particularly useful to Fr. Volpi. Bruno was the first to make public the decision of the Vatican to have Fr. Volpi appointed as apostolic commissioner over the Friars of the Immaculate and he informed journalists in a one-sided fashion. Some called him the head of the friars who sought to move the institute in the liberal direction.

During Father Volpi's "reign of terror," countless friars left
the official structure of the institute. Although detailed information about the order's current status remains difficult to obtain,
some estimates reckon that more than two thirds of the institute
tried to find another solution; many called for a re-founding. A
small group of friars requested to leave the institute, seeking
refuge in the Philippines. Six friars approached Archbishop
Ramon Cabrera Argüelles of Lipa, in the Philippines, to assess
the possibility of re-founding the institute with their original
charism within his diocese. These were tracked down by Father
Volpi and Father Bruno and punished with a suspension *a divinis*. Normally the request to leave a congregation, order, or
institute is common and is granted by the thousand for a wide
variety of reasons. In the case of the Friars of the Immaculate,
all the members were collectively blocked from leaving and
forced to live in atmosphere of suppression, an action with no
canonical support. Through all this, Father Volpi never clarified
what misconduct the order was guilty of.

Meanwhile Volpi's accusations against Father Manelli of
absconding with the order's property were tossed out by secular courts. Volpi had filed a lawsuit for suspicion of fraud,
forgery of documents, and embezzlement, and Father Manelli
answered these with a libel action against Father Volpi for
defamation. The courts ordered Father Volpi to return the
assets, fined him twenty thousand euros, and ordered him to
issue a public apology. In July 2015, the court of Avellino ruled
that there had been no misconduct of any kind by Father
Manelli or anyone else associated with the Friars of the Immaculate and ordered the release of property belonging to Mission

of the Immaculate Mediatrix (MIM) and the Third Order of the Franciscan Friars of the Immaculate (TOFI) that had been seized by Volpi. The value of the assets totaled about thirty million euros.

In the Philippines, Archbishop Ramon Cabrera Argüelles of Lipa, who had taken in six friars, offered them a *celebret*—permission to say Mass—in his archdiocese. Father Volpi's reaction was swift: he attended the Italian Bishops' Conference in autumn 2014 and urged the bishops not to incardinate priests seeking to leave the maltreated institute, even accusing the friars of a plot to "overthrow" the pope. In the meantime, Archbishop Cabrera Argüelles filed his resignation three years ahead of his mandatory retirement age, and it was accepted by Pope Francis in February 2017.

On April 4, 2016, the Congregation for Religious ruled, by the rescript *Ex audientia*, that bishops must consult with the Vatican before establishing an institute of diocesan right. This has been the only formal response to the affair from the pope, and it represents a bureaucratizing step. Many observers commented that this action had but one target: the diocese in the Philippines which had tried to make possible a re-founding of the Friars of the Immaculate.

The Sisters of the Immaculate

A year after the takeover of the friars, the Vatican turned its attention to the sisters. Cardinal Braz de Aviz ordered a visitation to be headed by Sister Fernanda Barbiero of the Institute of the Sisters of St. Dorothy, known for her moderately feminist tendencies within an "up-to-date" order. Sister Barbiero was given powers that equaled those of the friars' commissioner. But there was one important difference: while the visitation of the Friars had been caused by a small group of dissidents, the Sisters stood united against the visitation, nor had any complaint been sent to the Vatican.

Between May and July 2014 Sister Barbiero called for an additional two apostolic visitors—the Poor Clare prioresses Damiana Tiberio and Cristiana Mondonico, who reportedly held the Old Rite in a general attitude of disdain—to investigate the contemplative branch of the institute. The visitors told the nuns that they prayed too much and did too much penance! Also that they were "too cloistered" and needed a reeducation program according to the criteria of the Second Vatican Council.

The Sisters of the Immaculate filed an appeal to the Tribunal of the Apostolic Segnatura, still headed by Cardinal Raymond Burke who had attempted to defend the friars. The Segnatura concurred that the visitors had exceeded their authority, as described in canon law. Four months later Cardinal Burke was removed by Pope Francis from his position as head of the Segnatura.

What Was It All About?

On June 7, 2015, these extreme measures came to an unexpected halt: Father Fidenzio Volpi suffered a stroke. He was hospitalized immediately but died at eleven a.m. that day. The new commissioner chosen for the institute was the Salesian Father Sabino Ardito, a canon lawyer, who carried on the same task, but with a more moderate approach. At this writing, the full status of the order—including the numbers who remain—is unknown. The latest news is that at least fifteen of the Friars of the Immaculate houses have been closed, sixty brothers have officially asked to be released from their vows—it is not known how many have simply walked away—and at least some houses of the sisters are reported to be turning away vocations because of the crisis. The new commissioner is preparing to rewrite the order's constitutions to abolish the special consecration to Mary, a provision that had been approved by Pope John Paul II. It is also proposed to change the vow of absolute poverty so that the Order may in future own property; the object of this seems to be to enable the Vatican to control the Order through its property.

Father Volpi's letters and actions did provide clarification on one point: "The intervention in the Franciscans of the Immaculate was precipitated by their increasing attachment to *Traditional Catholic theological positions* not just to the Traditional Latin Mass." [Emphasis in the original.] While many Catholics attempted to minimize Pope Francis's involvement in the punishment of the Friars of the Immaculate, the continued Vatican-driven strictures applied against the order, particularly after so many interventions by the faithful appealing to the pope, can leave few in doubt.

The Vaticanist Sandro Magister wrote of the Catholic world's "astonishment" at the Vatican's attack on the order, saying "the Franciscans of the Immaculate are one of the most flourishing religious communities born in the Catholic Church in recent decades." But it is notable that the religious appointed to oversee the takeover were themselves members of congregations in precipitous decline, including the Capuchins of Father Volpi and the

Salesians of Father Ardito. While the Franciscans of the Immaculate grew exponentially in only a little over forty years, the Franciscan Friars Minor suffered a drop in vocations of 41 percent. It is worth asking if it was, in fact, the very success of the Friars of the Immaculate's more traditional approach that drew the wrath of the "progressives" whose fifty-year-long experiment seemed to have failed.

This speculation was repeated in September 2016 by the Vaticanist Giuseppe Nardi, who wrote that, for the progressives, "A new-rite order, which had moved to the traditional rite, attracted numerous vocations of young people and aroused growing attention from other new-rite orders, which began to be interested in this 'success story,' obviously ought not to exist." The destruction of the Friars of the Immaculate has been a message well received by these other orders, which have been careful to keep their heads down.

In all this Pope Francis's attitude has been characteristically opaque. He turned a deaf ear to the countless petitions and pleas from the friars and the faithful, but no formal canonical case was ever made against Father Manelli and the pope made no response when secular courts found against the commissioner he had set over the Friars of the Immaculate.

Pope Francis's treatment of the Franciscan Friars of the Immaculate should be compared to his treatment of the Legionaries of Christ. The former institute was founded by the saintly Manelli, who had all accusations against him overturned by the secular courts; the latter was founded by the sexually promiscuous drug addict Marcial Maciel, who devoted his time between his mistresses to amassing a fortune in donations from the wealthy.

Few bodies represented more than the Legionaries the alliance of the Church with capitalism against which Pope Francis has launched repeated condemnations. By contrast, the Franciscans of the Immaculate were infants in the world of ecclesiastical politics. Their following of St. Francis was a full one, in their genuine poverty, in their unworldly innocence, and in their dedication to a spiritual vocation. Here if anywhere was the "Church of the poor" which Pope Francis called for at the outset of his reign.

In the case of the Legionaries of Christ, the Church made public the allegations against the founder and explained what actions it was taking to achieve reform. Cardinal Velasio de Paolis, who was charged with investigating the Legion on behalf of Pope Benedict, behaved like a benevolent father towards the Legionaries, even though their charism was very different from his.

Benedict XVI did not punish the Congregation as a whole but carefully and meticulously tried to shed what was bad in the Legion and retain what was good. That was the line that Cardinal de Paolis followed. The investigation was long and difficult, but the Legion's constitutions were amended, and then approved by the Vatican in November 2014.

When Jorge Bergoglio was elected pope in 2013 he approved the investigation of the Friars of the Immaculate. No official charges were made against the founder, Father Stefano Manelli, and no evidence was produced. A campaign surfaced in the media to slander Father Manelli, who was punished with house arrest and allowed no opportunity to defend himself. At the same time his order was directed tyrannically by a Capuchin father who ran the order into the ground and set out from the beginning to destroy a significant element of the institute's charism, the Old Rite of the Mass.

Mirroring this difference in treatment one can only notice a difference in the worldly capacities of the two institutes. The Legionaries of Christ distinguished themselves from their foundation by their close rapport with rich donors and financial institutions. The lavish donations they made to the Vatican were surely one reason why the accusations against their founder were blocked and suppressed until Cardinal Joseph Ratzinger, first as prefect of the Congregation for the Doctrine of the Faith and then as Pope Benedict XVI, investigated the charges.[4] The facts speak for themselves. Pope Benedict investigated real crimes, handled them with justice and mercy, and began the process of reform of the Legion—with that reform at least tacitly approved by Pope Francis—while Pope Francis treated the innocent Friars of the Immaculate with a severity seldom meted out to any other order.

2. THE INTERVENTION IN THE ORDER OF MALTA

The "Order of Malta" is the name given today to the medieval order of the Knights Hospitaller. For five centuries the Order governed successively the islands of Rhodes and of Malta, which is why the latter name is given to it in common usage. Although the Order now operates from Rome, having surrendered Malta to Napoleon in 1798, the sovereignty it acquired has always (by a curious but fully accepted anomaly) continued to be recognized in international law: the Grand Master ranks as a sovereign prince, his ambassadors accredited to over a hundred countries have equal standing with those of other states, and the Order's headquarters in Rome enjoy extraterritorial status.[5] The knights nowadays devote themselves to their hospitaller tradition and run charitable agencies all over the world. The core of the Order is a small number of celibate knights who take the religious vows, as they did when they constituted a fighting elite in the Crusades, but the bulk of it consists of honorary knights and dames, organized in National Associations. At one time the Order represented the height of aristocratic exclusiveness, but that character has long been diluted; its composition ranges from the strictly aristocratic, as still seen in a few of the European associations, to countries where it has no nobiliary character at all.

The conflict which led to Pope Francis forcing the resignation of the Grand Master in January 2017 originated in a national rivalry which had come to a head with the previous election of the Order's governing Council. On the one side was the German Association, which is by far the richest of the Order's national groupings, receiving large subsidies from the German government; it is also highly efficient, and runs a number of charitable agencies, which include Malteser International. It was at loggerheads with the Grand Master, the Englishman Fra Matthew Festing,[6] whose office was a life appointment. Through bad electoral management by the Grand Master's supporters, and corresponding efficiency on the other side, the election of 2014 placed the Germans in a very strong position in the Order's government: three of the Council's ten members were from that country (Baron Boeselager, Count Esterhazy, and Count Henckel von Donnersmarck), while another two, both of them also noblemen, were nominees of the German lobby. On the other side were four councilors who were supporters of the Grand Master, with a tenth who might be called a floating voter. Five of the Council's number, in addition to the Grand Master, were professed knights who had taken vows of poverty, chastity, and obedience.

Grand Master Festing was an insular Englishman who, after being called to Italy by his election in 2008, had not made much progress with the language, and even less in mastering the labyrinth of Italian and Vatican political circles. Although he came from a distinguished military family, Fra Matthew was not an aristocrat, and it may be that his unassuming ways contributed to the hostility shown towards him by some of the Germans. Fra Matthew was also an out-and-out traditionalist, in doctrinal and liturgical terms, as were two or three of his supporters on the Council, and this in itself made for a lack of understanding between the two sides as regards their religious outlook. Not all of the latter councilors were professed knights, but all of them, in contrast to the five noblemen on the German side, were middle-class men who had taken the Order's centuries-old religious vocation as their inspiration. This was the aspect that the Grand Master was keen to promote, and in the nine years that he was in office he took measures to strengthen the spiritual life of the Order. He issued rules prescribing stricter religious obligations for the professed, set up an Institute of Spirituality, which published a Journal of Spirituality in yearly installments, and began courses of formation for professed knights and chaplains. When Fra Matthew Festing took over as Grand Master there were only some thirty professed knights, but he doubled their strength, raising them to some sixty members from different countries; it is striking that, despite constant urging, not one of these came from Germany. It may be added that the professed knights nowadays are mostly non-noble, which is one reason why the highly aristocratic German Association looks askance at them.

A Scandal in the Charitable Works

Over the years before 2017, Grand Master Festing received reports that the charitable agencies run by the German Association, including Malteser International, were covertly distributing condoms as part of their work in Asia, Africa, and elsewhere. This came under the responsibility of Baron Albrecht von Boeselager as Grand Hospitaller, a post he held until 2014. Grand Master Festing ordered an enquiry, which reported in 2016 that even if Boeselager had not directly ordered the distribution of condoms himself, he knew what was going on and failed to disclose it. In the meantime, however, Boeselager had been elected to the office of Grand Chancellor, which is that of prime minister of the Order. The Grand Master wanted a disciplinary proceeding against him for his actions as Grand Hospitaller, and he was supported in this by Cardinal Burke, who was patronus of the Order.[7]

In November 2016 Cardinal Burke had an audience with Pope Francis in which he explained the scandal of the condom distribution and asked for authorization to act against it. A letter from the pope on December 1 appeared to grant that authorization. On the subject of the condoms, it said: "Particular care will be taken that methods and means contrary to the moral law are not employed and distributed in charitable initiatives and relief efforts. If in the past some problems have arisen in this area, I hope that it can be completely resolved. I would be frankly displeased if, in fact, some senior Officials—as you yourself have told me—while knowing of these practices, especially regarding the distribution of contraceptives of any kind, have not hitherto intervened to put an end to it."[8]

This seemed a signal to go ahead. There were also parts of the letter which reflected Pope Francis's past experiences with the Order in Argentina, a background which needs to be explained. In 1997, Bergoglio and Bishop Héctor Aguer, as auxiliary bishops of Buenos Aires, were the two leading candidates to be named archbishop with automatic rights to succeed Cardinal Quarracino. Aguer was an honorary chaplain of the Knights of Malta, and an Argentinian politician, Esteban Caselli, who was a Knight of Malta and ambassador of the Order, used his Vatican links to try to get Aguer promoted to the archbishopric in preference to Bergoglio. When the latter was appointed instead, Caselli attempted a gesture of reconciliation by arranging for the government to send him a first-class ticket to Rome when he went there to receive the pallium, but Bergoglio returned it shredded to pieces.[9] The maneuvers of 1997 had not had any particular ideological tinge (Aguer seemed a more well-groomed and cultivated candidate, though not noticeably more conservative), but during the next fifteen years, as Bergoglio moved visibly to the Left, Caselli and Aguer emerged as the leading figures in the conservative opposition to him. The conflict had a recrudescence when Bergoglio's bad relations with the government of President Cristina Fernández de Kirchner (2007–2015) reached such a point that a group of bishops and laymen sought to replace him as archbishop of Buenos Aires. Bishop Aguer was not necessarily the alternative envisaged on this occasion, but Caselli, with his Vatican influence, was again the leading lay actor.

These events on his home soil had given Pope Francis an unusual experience of the Order of Malta. The Order is a decentralized organization, and its policy (if one can call it that) has always been to set up an Association in a country and leave it to carry on in its own way. The result is that in much of Latin America it has typically displayed a plutocratic character, with little attention to the charitable works in which it shines elsewhere; in other words, it represented the sort of right-wing, capitalistic Catholicism against which Bergoglio's rhetoric was habitually directed.

In Argentina, there was another odd twist involving a scandal with the Knights, and, curiously, the Masons. A scandal involving the Italian pseudo-Masonic lodge P2 reached its climax in the 1990s after the leader of the lodge was found murdered by Mafia enemies. The number two man in the lodge was the banker Umberto Ortolani, who was imprisoned for fraudulent bankruptcy. Ortolani also happened to be a Knight of Malta (having concealed his membership in P2), and was even an ambassador of the Order in Latin America; and nowhere was the P2 more active outside of Italy than in Argentina.

These past misdeeds help to explain some remarks in the pope's letter to Cardinal Burke which had little relevance to the issue that had been raised with him. The pope alluded to "manifestations of a worldly spirit which are contrary to the Catholic faith" and warned against "affiliations and associations, movements and organizations"—such as Freemasonry, which had always been something of a bee in Bergoglio's bonnet.

Armed with the pope's letter, Cardinal Burke presented himself at the Order's headquarters in Rome and announced that the time had come to take action over the condom scandal. The initial idea was to bring a disciplinary proceeding against Boese-lager, which would have implied his suspension while the charges were investigated; but this required a two-thirds majority in the Order's Council, which was blocked by the German party. The Grand Master therefore chose, in an exceptional use of his power as a religious superior, to demand Boeselager's resignation under the promise that he had taken as a Knight of Obedience (a special class of the Order, qualifying a non-professed knight to hold the higher offices). On Boeselager's refusal, on December 8, 2016, the Grand Master dismissed him, technically for breach of the promise of obedience. No claim was made (as some later alleged) that the pope had explicitly ordered Boeselager's dismissal, but his letter seemed a guarantee that the papal backing was there for the Grand Master's action.

Follow the Money

Across this dispute, however, which was a moral and disci-plinary one, fell another affair which explains the extraordinary intervention now made by the Vatican. It concerns a large trust fund which had been set up years before by a French donor, with the intention that part of it should go on his death to the Order of Malta. By 2013 the fund was being managed by a trustee in Geneva who was well known for handling a range of trusts in tax havens and the like. The names of the Swiss fund and the trustee are perfectly well known and have been published, but they are not mentioned here because of the threats of legal action that the trustee promptly made to preserve her anonymity. It can be stated however that in 2013, under the previous Grand Chancellor, the Order began a lawsuit against the trustee over her management of the trust, and other potential beneficiaries were associated in the case, including the Hospitaller Order of St. John of God. They made a complaint to the public prosecutor, who responded by freezing the assets of the trust.

In 2014, however, when Boeselager became Grand Chancellor he decided on a different approach. With the help of two bankers (who were Knights of Malta and professionally active in Switzerland) and the papal nuncio in Geneva, Archbishop Silvano Tomasi who was on friendly terms with the trustee, Grand Chancellor Boeselager advocated a halt to the lawsuit against the trustee; in return, she would release an agreed portion of the funds to the Knights. To what extent the Holy See stood to benefit is a disputed point. It seems clear that Archbishop Tomasi expected money from the trust; and it is thought that the Vatican expected Boeselager to provide it with a portion of the money that the Order of Malta was to receive. It has even been alleged that the Vatican was waiting to quash the Order's sovereign status and take over its assets lock, stock, and barrel.

Boeselager's plan, however, came up against the opposition of Grand Master Festing, who wanted the lawsuit to run its course. This had the hidden snag (although he was not aware of it) that the trustee was threatening to reveal all the communications she had had with Boeselager and his associates if she came under judicial interrogation, a fate that could only be avoided if a compromise was reached. As a final touch, the deadline for the criminal prosecution was the end of January 2017.

The Vatican Intervenes

What this meant was that the dismissal of Boeselager on December 8 precipitated a real crisis, and it was one that had nothing to do with the distribution of condoms. Without him as Grand Chancellor, there was no hope of stopping the lawsuit by January; various parties would not get the money they were hoping for, and a quantity of embarrassing private communications would see the light of day. Fortunately (from his point of view), Boeselager was in a good position to pull strings. As it happened, his brother George had just been appointed to the Cardinals' Commission for Oversight of the Institute for Works of Religion, the appointment being announced on December 15; in other words, he had become one of the governors of the Vatican Bank. Albrecht Boeselager himself was well known to be thick as thieves with Cardinal Parolin, the secretary of state; in fact, in April 2017 a German Knight of Malta revealed that the two had been working together for the past two years to undermine Cardinal Burke's position in the Order. Archbishop Tomasi also had, of course, a hotline to the secretary of state. Within days, the Vatican apparatus swung into action to overturn the inopportune dismissal. Cardinal Parolin wrote the Grand Master a heated letter arguing that the pope's intentions were to be understood in a context of dialogue, and that he never intended the dismissal of anyone (an assertion that became ironical in the light of what soon happened). But the Grand Master and Cardinal Burke, who were interpreting the pope's attitude in the light of his letter of December 1, saw no reason to give way. Stronger measures would be necessary on Cardinal Parolin's side, and they took the form of an action which was supremely revealing. On December 22, Parolin announced the appointment of a commission (euphemistically styled a "group") to study the dismissal of the Grand Chancellor. It consisted of Archbishop Tomasi as president, the two bankers who had been involved in the business of the Swiss fund, a decrepit Belgian Knight of Malta who was an unconditional partisan of Boeselager's, and a Curial Jesuit whose qualification for his post, to judge from his pronouncements during the following investigation, may have been a bland indifference to the morality of the use of condoms.

The first point to be made about this act is one of jurisdiction. In 1952, when a dispute had arisen between the Order of Malta and the Holy See, Pope Pius XII personally appointed a special commission of five cardinals to try it, since nothing less would have been due to the Order's sovereign character; yet here it was proposed, on the authority of the secretary of state, to have five persons of no status judging the actions of the Grand Master of the Order (Festing) and the cardinal (Burke) on whose advice he had acted. The second fault was the glaring conflict of interest of at least three of the commissioners named, Archbishop Tomasi and the two bankers; indeed it is astonishing that Cardinal Parolin wantonly directed attention in this way to the real point of conflict, a link that was immediately picked up by the press: if nothing else, it showed what *he* thought the real problem was. And the third anomaly was the mismatch between the professed aim of the commission—to investigate the dismissal of the Grand Chancellor—and what it proceeded to do. On January 7, 2017, Archbishop Tomasi circulated a letter to members of the Order, most of whom had no knowledge of the circumstances of Boeselager's dismissal, inviting them to submit whatever information they pleased, with the unstated hope of eliciting complaints against the management of Grand Master Festing. The commission performed its work with indecent haste, and was to produce, well before its appointed deadline of the end of January, a viciously defamatory report that was exclusively the work of the Grand Master's enemies.

Under this onslaught, the response of the Grand Magistry was ineffectual from the start. After dismissing Boeselager, Fra Matthew Festing had gone off to England for his Christmas holidays. Alone at home, he issued a series of aggressive declarations that left a bad impression. Meanwhile, in Rome, the post of Grand Chancellor had been transferred to the senior knight available, Fra John Critien, who had until then been curator of the Order's art collections; he was an amiable man, but with no experience of diplomacy or of law. In response to the attacks on the Grand Master he issued a defense written by the Order's official lawyer. In the form published—it badly needed editing—it was obscure and inept and did not help the Grand Master's cause. On December 23, the Grand Master sent a letter to the pope, couched in respectful terms, pointing out why the appointment of Cardinal Parolin's commission was "unacceptable"—a word that was picked up as evidence of intransigence, with the press reporting that a "sharp conflict" had arisen between the Order of Malta and the pope. Yet it should be realized that Fra

Matthew Festing had no such idea in his head. He imagined that he had the pope's support in the action to punish the condom distribution, and that he was simply resisting an intervention that Cardinal Parolin had made for reasons of his own. Equally unwarranted was the idea of a fundamental clash between a hard-line moral stance on the part of the Grand Master and Cardinal Burke, and the more "merciful" policy being pursued by Pope Francis. His letter of December 1, condemning "contraceptives of any kind" as "contrary to the moral law" seemed clear enough—unless he had changed his mind since then.

During the seven weeks until Pope Francis forced Fra Matthew's resignation, the Order defended its right to conduct its government in its own way. Some accused the Order of arrogance in asserting its sovereignty against the Holy See; but it is natural to assert rights that have been respected in the past. In its definitive judgment of February 19, 1953, the Holy See itself had ruled that the Order of Malta, as a religious order, was subject to the jurisdiction of the Congregation for Religious, but it also recognized the Order as a sovereign political entity. There was no suggestion that the Secretariat of State (which is responsible for the Holy See's diplomatic relations with sovereign governments) had any jurisdiction over the Order, nor had it claimed any such right.

In 2017, however, no attempt was made to refer the case to the Congregation of Religious, the proper competent body. Cardinal Parolin as secretary of state claimed an authority over the Order as absolute as if it had been a parish council. His disregard for the law was quickly matched by that of the pope himself. On January 23, he summoned Fra Matthew Festing to come the Vatican, informing nobody and bringing nobody with him. In their audience the following afternoon he demanded Fra Matthew's immediate resignation, while Baron Boeselager was to be reinstated as Grand Chancellor. Thus, in an astonishing papal intervention, the man suspected of flouting the Church's moral teaching was rewarded, and the superior who had tried to discipline him lost his office.

What Was behind It?

One need hardly point out how disproportionate the dismissal of the Grand Master was to the case: even if Fra Matthew had behaved mistakenly in dismissing Boeselager, was his resignation the fitting penalty? But in fact the measure has an easy, and even absurd, explanation. Fra Matthew Festing had the values of his British military background, and he had been indignant that Boeselager refused to resign when asked. A gentleman, he held, would do the decent thing in such a case and go without waiting to be pushed. In the weeks before January 24, he had been saying openly in the magistral palace: "If the Pope asked me to resign I would do so." He said this not because he had any notion that it might happen—for at that time he imagined that he was acting with the pope's support—but as a point of personal conduct. But, like everything said in the Palazzo Malta, his remark was quickly known in the Vatican; the pope was told, and he immediately saw an easy victory. Thus he asked for Fra Matthew's resignation on January 24 because he knew in advance that he would get it.

Some in the press portrayed this turn of events as a victory of a populist pope over an aristocratic religious order, but the actual effect of Pope Francis's intervention was to support an aristocratic *coup d'état* in the Order of Malta. This can be shown simply by reciting the names of the German members of the Order's Council: Baron Albrecht von Boeselager, Count Janos Esterhazy, and Count Winfried Henckel von Donnersmarck,[10] backed by the president of the German Association, Prince Erich Lobkowicz, and his brother Johannes. It is they who are now in the saddle, while the other party in the Order—the non-noble members of the Council who supported the Grand Master—has gone into eclipse. It is a picture exactly opposite to that of a papal blow against privilege that was drawn by some journalists.

But the most significant aspect of the pope's action was that it undermined Cardinal Burke, against whom Pope Francis had been mobilizing covert subversion ever since Burke had signed the *dubia* of the previous December seeking clarification on *Amoris laetitia*. Burke's function as cardinal patronus of the Order of Malta was suspended, while Archbishop Becciu was appointed a special Delegate to direct the Order in place of the Grand Master, in total disregard for its sovereign status. The personal significance of the upheaval was even clearer: at a stroke, the departure of Fra Matthew Festing removed Cardinal Burke's most like-minded ally in the Order of Malta and put it under the control of Boeselager, his declared enemy, who had protested bitterly against his appointment as patronus in 2014.

A Decapitated Order

Pope Francis's intervention was carried through with familiar methods. The resignation of the Grand Master still required, under the Order's constitution, approval by the Council; on January 25, the day after Fra Matthew's resignation, the acting Grand Chancellor received a telephone call from Archbishop Becciu, in the pope's name, warning him against any last-ditch stand. On the same day a Curial prelate, with no office in the Order but well-disposed to it, arrived to give private advice. He confided to the knights: "You need to realize that Pope Francis is a ruthless and vindictive dictator, and if you make the slightest attempt at resistance he will destroy the Order."

Heeding these warnings, on January 28, the Council of the Order, with the Grand Master still present, voted for surrender: Fra Matthew's resignation was accepted, Fra John Critien stepped down as Grand Chancellor, and Baron Boeselager resumed his place, appearing in the council room as soon as the Grand Master left it. Within days of his reinstatement, Boeselager stopped the lawsuit against the trustee in Geneva, in the nick of time. The Order has received thirty million euros from the trust, and Archbishop Tomasi is reported to have been paid one hundred thousand Swiss francs for his foundation Caritas in Veritate. As for the condom affair, Boeselager's denials of responsibility have been accepted without scrutiny, and he is the man effectively in control of the Order.

Since then, the Vatican's pressure on the Order has continued undiminished. In his conversation with the pope on January 24, Grand Master Festing had agreed to resign on the understanding that a normal election would be held to choose his successor. He even asked the pope, "What if they re-elect me?" and Pope Francis had said that would be acceptable. This reply was reported by Fra Matthew to the knight attending him in the car returning from the Vatican, and it was known to everyone in the magistral palace the same evening. In the event, the election in late April was held under close Vatican supervision, including an attempt to prevent Fra Matthew from taking part in it, as was his right as a Bailiff Grand Cross of the Order; it was made clear that his reelection would not be tolerated. The outcome was the election of a nonentity to head the Order, not as Grand Master but as interim Lieutenant for twelve months, as the best cover for the continued control of Boeselager (who, not being professed, was not himself eligible). This result was obtained in the face of widespread concern in the Order over many of the problems that had been revealed: the shady financial background of the crisis, the arbitrary intervention of the Vatican, the injustice to Fra Matthew Festing, the brushing under the carpet of the condom scandal, and the secularization of the Order likely to be entailed by the "reforms" spoken of by Boeselager and the German party.[11]

Pope Francis's intervention in the Order of Malta falls within the familiar pattern of his methods: as regards Cardinal Burke, an initial conversation in which he gave an impression of support, followed by comprehensive betrayal, aimed at humiliating an opponent; as regards the Grand Master, a private summons to come alone to an audience, telling no one, and a surprise demand for resignation. Linked with this is the cavalier attitude to the moral teaching of the Church, but a very practical appreciation of money and power, which sits uneasily with the aspirations of a "Church of the poor" and the condemnations of "spiritual worldliness."

Nevertheless, unlike the Friars of the Immaculate, the Order of Malta has not suffered in personal terms from the blow to its government. What has suffered is the rule of law. Within days of the dismissal of the Grand Master a chorus of criticism arose, notably from lawyers, against what the pope had done. It was pointed out that, if the Holy See could ride roughshod over the sovereignty of the Order of Malta, there was nothing to stop the government of Italy from sending in its police to investigate the finances of Vatican City. Many suspect that this realization stopped Pope Francis and Cardinal Parolin from taking over the Order unconditionally, as their initial declarations suggested. It was a characteristic feature in an episode in which the considerations of power and financial control were to the fore and morality was in slight regard.

Chapter 6

KREMLIN SANTA MARTA

I n early 2017, English journalist Damian Thompson wrote: "It is not hard to detect a Latin American flavour to the deal-making and settling of scores that has become blatant over the past year" in the regime of Pope Francis.[1] Actually, this flavor had been present from the beginning where his own country was concerned. Before his election, Cardinal Bergoglio had been in conflict with a religious group, the Institute of the Incarnate Word, which had been founded in Argentina thirty years before and had proved highly successful, attracting many vocations. It was opposed by elements in the national hierarchy who felt challenged by a movement of conservative character, but Benedict XVI had overruled them, dismissing the Argentinian bishops' case in 2009. Within days of his election, Pope Francis reopened it and soon sent the founder of the institute, Father Buela, into exile in Spain.

Two members of the Argentinian hierarchy also felt the new wind blowing. In 2014, Monsignor José Luis Mollaghan was dismissed as archbishop of Rosario on the grounds that he was in disagreement with his clergy, and the following year Monsignor Oscar Sarlinga was removed as bishop of Zárate supposedly for economic difficulties in his diocese. What they had in common was that in 2011, as Cardinal Bergoglio's seventy-fifth birthday approached, they had written a letter to Rome urging that his retirement be accepted immediately.

Another figure to receive short shrift was the Argentinian by birth Rogelio Livieres, bishop of Ciudad del Este in Paraguay. He had founded a seminary which gained enormous success, attracting students from all over South America, including a few from Bergoglio's own seminary in Buenos Aires. During Livieres's time in office, his diocese showed a spectacular increase in every aspect of religious activity; the number of diocesan priests alone leapt from fourteen to eighty-three. It is true that Livieres made a serious mistake: he promoted a foreign priest, deceived by what a previous superior described as "his brilliant, charismatic personality," and ignoring the fact that the man had been accused in his earlier career of molesting seminarians. But in fact this error of judgment was not an accusation that Pope Francis made against Bishop Livieres;[2] what he alleged was that Livieres was in conflict with the rest of the Paraguayan hierarchy—how should he not be, considering what they were? In September 2014 Bishop Livieres was dismissed; his seminary was dispersed and his exceptional work in South America was destroyed. Reflecting on these acts, one may admit that some popes—very rare ones—have come to the throne with an impatience of certain ecclesiastical problems they had run into in their time and have dealt with them summarily. But a connoisseur of papal minutiae would have to rack his brain to find anything that quite matches the cases outlined above: the Curial shake-up ordered by Paul VI (1963–1978), the anti-Modernist drive of Pius X (1903–1914)? They hardly fit the same pattern of apparent personal reprisals. The fact is that no pope in modern times has come to the throne in bad relations with so many people as Jorge Bergoglio did; and his predecessors were as a rule sufficiently high-minded to avoid any action that might look like unworthy revenge.

The New Regime of Casa Santa Marta

When Pope Francis was elected, no act of his was more praised, as showing his fresh, democratic spirit, than the decision to avoid the old papal apartment in the Apostolic Palace and move into quarters in Casa Santa Marta, the well-appointed guesthouse for visiting cardinals, where he has lived ever since. Other implications of this choice have been somewhat overlooked, for example the fact that upgrading the Casa Santa Marta for its new purpose is said to have cost two million euros—while the old papal apartment of course still has to be kept up. But it is worth assessing the psychological aspects of the move. Omar Bello notes that Pope Francis took one look at the old apartment, with its stately suites, where the popes had traditionally eaten their meals in grave solitude, and immediately realized that it isolated the pope from the Curia. In Santa Marta, Pope Francis has the cardinals close to him, and he eats in the public dining room. A journalist has pointed out that this serves as a "method of control, in order to get informed at lunch about the happenings in the diverse camps in the Vatican."[3] The tight grip that Cardinal Bergoglio kept over his archiepiscopal Curia in Buenos Aires is thus transferred to his new position.

The regime that Pope Francis conducts from this stronghold is one in which the expectations of reform have been dashed and replaced by a chaos where even his closest associates feel insecure. Initially, he rewarded the two men who served as his agents in Rome while he was archbishop in Buenos Aires: Monsignor Guillermo Karcher and Monsignor Fabián Pedacchio. Pedacchio became a sort of informal papal secretary, succeeded the official holder of that position (the Maltese Monsignor Xuereb) in 2014, and has remained in favor, at least for now. But Karcher, who at first basked in his dignity as papal *cerimoniere,* now seems to have lost the pope's favor and has been sidelined. The *udienza di tabella,* which assured heads of dicasteries twice-monthly audiences, has been abolished, and access to the papal presence is left to the whim of Pope Francis. Bishops who work in the Vatican will tell you that the old fraternal meetings which the popes used to grant them have disappeared; some of them have hardly spoken to Francis since he was elected. Nothing could be less "collegial" than the way this hero of the St. Gallen lobby treats his subordinates. The control of the Secretariat of State over the rest of the Curia has become more absolute than ever. And everyone, from cardinals to monsignori, is kept in a state of permanent nerves by the naggings, the brusque public criticisms, the sackings, and the covert undermining that are the hallmark of the new regime.

Cardinal Pietro Parolin, appointed secretary of state in October 2013, was at first the Curial favorite, and was indulged by

Francis in his determination to preserve and even extend the prerogatives of his office. But it is not Francis's style to leave anyone secure. For some time now the pope has been using Parolin's *sostituto*, Archbishop Angelo Becciu, as a more ready tool, because he has more to gain from his master. Becciu is the man who does the pope's dirty jobs for him, and he does them efficiently. It was he who telephoned PricewaterhouseCoopers in 2015 to inform them that the Vatican audit would not be coming near the Secretariat of State; he was the man imposed on the Knights of Malta in Francis's heavy-handed takeover of that order; and he was the key figure in the dismissal of the Vatican's auditor general in June 2017. It is widely thought in the Vatican that Becciu now has more real power than Parolin, and he may well be stepping into his shoes soon.[4] All in all, what we have here is a regime every bit as political and unspiritual as what was seen under Parolin's predecessors as secretary of state, Cardinals Bertone and Sodano.

In this regime, the prelates who enjoy favor are sycophants like Cardinal Coccopalmerio, who used his influence to protect the child-molesting priest Mauro Inzoli and who employed as his secretary Monsignor Luigi Capozzi, until he was arrested in a homosexual drugs party. Or an unreformed wheeler-dealer like Cardinal Calcagno, whose murky past as bishop of Savona does not disqualify him from being in charge of the Church's wealth. Or Cardinal Baldisseri, the skillful manipulator of "mercy" in the Synod on the Family.

On the other side, the cardinals who have felt the chill are those in whom Pope Benedict XVI placed his trust: Cardinals Burke, Müller, and Sarah, to whom one may add Cardinal Ouellet, who has now been sidelined because he shows himself too independent.[5] Setting aside ideology, these are all men who are sincere in word and action, and against whose moral character no word has been spoken. Those around Pope Francis are usually described by commentators as the "reformers," and the excluded ones as "anti-reform." It raises the question: how do we assess this reform that involves employing the devious and banishing the open and straightforward?

Cassock and Dagger in the Curia

The English journalist Damian Thompson quotes a priest who works in the Curia, and who started as a fervent supporter of Pope Francis, saying: "Bergoglio divides the Church into those who are with him and those who are against him—and if he thinks you're in the latter camp then he'll come after you."[6] This was the experience of three priests in the Congregation for the Doctrine of the Faith. In the summer of 2016 they were called up before the pope in person, accused of making unfavorable remarks about him and dismissed.[7] Cardinal Müller tried to defend them, and, in an audience which he obtained after several months of trying, protested to Francis: "These persons are among the best of my dicastery...what did they do?" The pope rebuffed his protests and closed the audience with the words: "And I am the Pope, I do not need to give reasons for any of my decisions. I have decided that they have to leave and they have to leave."[8]

Cardinal Müller himself, as the *ex officio* watchdog of Catholic orthodoxy, incurred the pope's disfavor for his opposition to the modification of the Church's teaching on marriage. After a number of slights over four years, in which he was effectively replaced with Cardinal Schönborn as the official doctrinal authority, Cardinal Müller was sent into retirement in July 2017, at the end of his five-year term. The failure to renew his mandate contrasts with normal practice, as does his retirement at the age of sixty-nine (while Cardinal Coccopalmerio, for example, continues to enjoy the pope's patronage at seventy-nine).[9] It is also worth noting that his replacement in the Congregation, Archbishop Ladaria, has been accused of protecting a priest who molested boys.

Even more drastic, in some ways, was the treatment meted out to Cardinal Robert Sarah, prefect of the Congregation for Divine Worship. Pope Francis appointed him to that post in November 2014 and instructed him at the time to continue in the liturgical line marked out by Pope Benedict XVI.[10] His downfall came when, in July 2016, speaking to a conference in London, he urged the restoration of the traditional practice of the priest celebrating the Mass *ad orientem*—that is, facing "east" (toward the altar). Contrary to what is usually supposed, no order has ever been given that the priest should say the Mass facing the people; it was a practice introduced in the 1960s, when it was believed that that was the usage of the early Church, an idea that is now known to be wrong. The point had been made by Cardinal Ratzinger as far back as 1993, when he was prefect of the Congregation for the Faith, and was familiar from his liturgical writings in general. Instructing the Church about liturgical authenticity is supposed to be one of the functions of the Congregation for Divine Worship; but Cardinal Sarah's words were received with protests from those who assumed that the practice of the past fifty years is unquestionable.

Letters protesting Cardinal Sarah's remarks arrived in Rome while he was away for the summer. Without allowing him the opportunity to deal with them, the secretary of the Congregation for Divine Worship, Archbishop Arthur Roche, took the letters to Pope Francis, who is not known for his expertise in liturgical matters, and he acted from knowledge of only one side of the question, the ignorant side. His reaction was perhaps the nearest to a Stalinist purge that the Vatican has seen. In October almost all the members of the Congregation for Divine Worship, many of whom had been appointed by Benedict XVI and followed his liturgical line, were ordered out in an unprecedented mass dismissal, and twenty-seven new members were named to take their places, thus leaving Cardinal Sarah entirely isolated.[11] He was obliged to cancel his attendance at a liturgical conference at which he had been due to speak on "The meaning of the *Motu Proprio Summorum Pontificum* for the renewal of the liturgy in the Latin Church." This action against Cardinal Sarah falls into a pattern of Pope Francis's giving one set of assurances to an official he appoints, before performing a *volte-face*; and also of his attacking those whom he sees as enemies not by dismissing them but by undermining them and leaving them powerless. As for Archbishop Roche, his reward for his intervention was that he is now the person who rules the roost in the Congregation for Divine Worship.

The watchword of the St. Gallen Group was the liberalization of the Church, and with their candidate in power we now see what it means. An attitude of pious horror at anyone who shows dissent from the papal line is the ruling orthodoxy. When the four cardinals, Brandmüller, Burke, Caffarra, and Meisner, signed a letter requesting clarification of the ambiguities in *Amoris laetitia*, the Dean of the Sacred Rota, Archbishop Vito Pinto, made the pronouncement: "What these cardinals have done is a very grave scandal which could lead the Holy Father to deprive them of the cardinal's hat.... One cannot doubt the action of the Holy Spirit."[12] For his part, Cardinal Blase Cupich of Chicago (who received the red hat in October 2016 in preference to several other American prelates whom many thought more obvious choices) declared that the cardinals were "in need of conversion." In a different field, Archbishop Rino Fisichella, the president of the Council for the New Evangelization, opened the Year of Mercy by suggesting that those who criticize the pope should incur the excommunication prescribed by canon law for those who offer physical violence to the pontiff, on the grounds that "words too are rocks and stones."[13] That is the way to get on in Pope Francis's Church, and the lesson is being well learnt.

The Thought-Police of Liberalism

The obsequious following of the papal line is not confined to a few toadies in the Curia; it has become policy in distant outposts of the Church. One may quote the fate of some of the forty-five signatories of a letter which was addressed on June 29, 2016, to the cardinals and patriarchs, asking them to petition the pope to correct a list of questionable propositions implied by the exhortation *Amoris laetitia*. One of the signatories was quickly dismissed from his position as a director of academic affairs at a pontifical university, after pressure from his archbish-opric. Another, who is a Dominican, was forbidden by his religious superior to speak publicly about the papal exhortation; a third was ordered to rescind his signature, and a cardinal put pressure on a fourth to withdraw his name.[14]

It may be pointed out that both the cardinals' *dubia* and the letter just mentioned took the form of requests for clarification, not of opposition; they may be contrasted with the open rejections of papal rulings that have been made without reprisal by "progressive" theologians in modern times, for example on the ordination of women. But under Pope Francis it has become an offense to ask for explanations. One may call to mind his own condemnation in *Evangelii gaudium* (2013) of authoritarians who "discredit those who raise questions, constantly point out the mistakes of others and are obsessed by appearances." There are people who have a talent for criticizing their own defects.

A sign of the times in Rome is a body calling itself the Osservatorio per l'Attuazione della Riforma della Chiesa di Papa Francesco (Observatory for the Implementation of the Church Reform of Pope Francis). As Sandro Magister reported in November 2016, at the beginning of that academic year this club of enthusiasts sent an email to the teaching staff of the Pontifical John Paul II Institute for Studies on Marriage and the Family. It noted:

> As has already occurred in other Catholic pastoral, academic and cultural institutions, our Observatory for the Implementation of the Church Reform of Pope

Francis—an initiative of Catholic lay people in support of the pontificate of Pope Francis—has begun in the current academic year the monitoring of the contents of the publications of faculty and the teachings imparted in the Pontifical John Paul II Institute for Studies on Marriage and the Family in order to make clear the adaptations or possible disagreements regarding the address made by Pope Francis on the occasion of the opening of the new academic year of your Institute (Sala Clementina, October 28, 2016), in which you were called "to support the necessary opening of the intelligence of the faith in the service of the pastoral solicitude of the successor of Peter."

In particular, the contents of published works, and the imparted classes will be taken into consideration in reference to what is expressed in the apostolic Exhortation "Amoris laetitia," according to the image "of the Church that is, not of a Church thought in one's own image and likeness," orienting research and teaching no longer towards "a too abstract theological ideal of matrimony, almost artificially built, far from the concrete situation and from the effective possibilities of families as they are" (Pope Francis, aforementioned address, October 28, 2016).

To this end, we will make use of the analytical and critical reading of the studies published by the faculty, of graduation and doctoral theses approved by the Institute, of the syllabus of classes, of their bibliographies, as well as interviews with students made after classes, in the square in front of the Lateran University.

Certain that we are performing a useful task to improve the service that you perform with dedication to the Church and to the Holy Father, we keep you up to date on the results of our observational study.[15]

The significance of this "observational study" is, of course, that the John Paul II Institute is the academic body that was set up to preserve that pontiff's teaching on the family, for which the present incumbent feels no enthusiasm.

As Sandro Magister points out, there is a precedent for such a posse of papal zealots in the Catholic world: it is the Sodalitium Pianum which was formed in the reign of Pius X (1903–1914) to enforce that pope's condemnation of Modernism. It acted by monitoring the lectures of seminary professors and reporting to the authorities any utterances that seemed to fall short of orthodoxy, and it has been reviled ever since by liberals as an example of the intellectual reign of terror introduced by Pius X. In general terms, one might think it a shame that our own days should have produced an echo of what was hitherto considered the most restrictive pontificate of modern times; but the irony goes further. It is no doubt natural that a regime that insists on strict orthodoxy should be backed, however regrettably, by measures that savor of a police state; but the "Observatory" of this modern Big Brother has sprung up in the reign of the progressive, liberal Pope Francis, elected by the open minds of St. Gallen to sweep back the alleged authoritarianism of Benedict XVI and John Paul II.

The Dictatorship of Mercy

Journalists covering Roman affairs are becoming increasingly aware that "under Pope Francis, the Vatican is systematically silencing, eliminating and replacing critics of the Pope's views."[16] Gianluigi Nuzzi reports that in March 2015 extensive bugging was discovered in the cars, offices, and private homes of Vatican clergy, and in an unexplained anomaly the Gendarmeria (the Vatican's internal security service) was not called in to investigate.[17] Clergy and laymen working in the Curia take it for granted that their telephone calls and their emails are being systematically spied on—and apparently with good reason.[18]

Few are willing to risk the pope's wrath by speaking freely on the phone or committing their frank thoughts to email. Damian Thompson reports that Pope Francis's outbursts of temper, his rudeness towards subordinates, and his vulgar language have become notorious throughout the Vatican. Thompson quotes a well-placed source: "Francis doesn't have to stand for re-election by the Conclave. Which, believe me, is lucky for him, because after the misery and nonsense of the past couple of years he'd be eliminated in the first ballot."[19] This is a truth that few in the Curia would doubt; they have woken up to the fact that the election of "The Great Reformer" in 2013 has had the effect of putting them under an old-style Argentinian dictatorship. Inspired by Francis's early public-relations antics, the Curia's original nickname for their reverend master was "Toto the Clown." They have now realized that they underestimated him. His current nickname is "Ming," after Ming the Merciless, the cruel emperor in the Flash Gordon comics. One cardinal has remarked: "In the Vatican, everybody fears Pope Francis; nobody respects him, from Cardinal Parolin down."

Fear is the dominant note in the Curia under Francis's rule, together with mutual mistrust. It is not simply the informers who curry favor by reporting unguarded talk—as Cardinal Müller's three subordinates discovered. In an organization in which the morally corrupt have been left in place, and even promoted by Pope Francis, subtle blackmail is the order of the day. One Curial priest has quipped: "They say it's not what you know but whom you know. In the Vatican that isn't true: it's what you know about whom you know."

This state of affairs is unprecedented in the Roman Curia, but we can read Austen Ivereigh's biography of Pope Francis to find a time and place where it was familiar. Describing the Perón regime of Bergoglio's youth, he tells how after 1952 "Perón became defensive and paranoid, descending into the authoritarian madness that commonly afflicts populist-nationalist governments in Latin America...state officials were required to be party members, disagreement was framed as dissent, and opponents...defined as enemies of the people."[20] Ivereigh does not note the parallel, but some elements of it can be found later in his narrative. When he moves on to Francis's pontificate, he presents a sketch of his Vatican "reforms" which may be called a masterpiece of spin, but even amid the propaganda, signs peep through of how autocratic and unpopular the pope's methods are: "Francis has arrogated to a close circle around him what used to be dealt with by Vatican institutions, and the circumventing of old channels causes great resentment. Francis's extraordinary popularity beyond the borders of the Church is in striking contrast to the view of him in the Vatican, where there is considerable grumbling.... It is a Bergoglio paradox: the collegial pope, close to the people, exercises his sovereign authority in ways that can seem high-handed. His is a highly personalistic government, which bypasses systems, depends on close relationships, works through people rather than documents, and keeps a tight control.... In many ways Francis is the most centralized pope since Pius the Ninth."[21]

Pius IX (1846–1878) and the days of the Papal States are indeed recalled by a phenomenon which had not been seen for many generations. On February 4, 2017, Romans woke up to find their city plastered with images mocking the pope.[22] These posters depicted Francis in one of his less jovial moods, and below him the legend: *A France', hai commissariato Congregazioni, rimosso sacerdoti, decapitato l'Ordine di Malta e i Francescani dell' Immacolata, ignorato Cardinali...ma n'do sta la tua misericordia?* This could be translated: "Hey, Frankie, you've busted Congregations, removed priests, decapitated the Order of Malta and the Franciscans of the Immaculate, ignored Cardinals...where's that mercy of yours, then?"

The squib, composed in the Romanesco dialect (the Roman Cockney), consciously recalled the pasquinades that used to appear in the days of the Temporal Power; and one would have to go back to those days to find the last case of a political satire against a reigning pope publicly displayed in Rome. This is one of several signs that the alleged popularity of Francis has plummeted in Italy and beyond. Another is that the number of people attending the more or less weekly papal audiences in St. Peter's Square had plunged. The official statistics for average attendance at these events since Francis became pope are:

2013: 51,617

2014: 27,883

2015: 14,818

For 2016 no figures have been made available, but they are understood to be under ten thousand: less than one-fifth of what they were four years ago, and in Benedict XVI's time.[23] To those who see the dwindling bands within St. Peter's colonnade, the message is clear: the People's Pope is being deserted by the people. Under his pontificate, Mass attendance is falling in Italy, and in much of the rest of the world. Francis's pontificate, which was expected to revivify the Church, after five years of hype is proving an unrelieved failure.

The Political Pope

It seems that Pope Francis himself has begun to realize the dangerous ground into which his "mess-creating" philosophy (*"Hagan lío"*) is taking him. He is reported to have remarked just before Christmas 2016: "It is not impossible that I will go down in history as the one who split the Catholic Church."[24] The thought has not escaped those around him, and in March 2017 the British newspaper the *Times* published an article under the headline "Anti-reform cardinals 'want the Pope to quit.'"[25] The article quoted Italian journalist Antonio Socci: "A large part of the cardinals who voted for him are very worried and the curia…which organised his election and has accompanied him thus far, without ever dissociating itself from him, is cultivating the idea of a moral suasion to persuade him to retire."[26] These "anti-reform" cardinals (note the media orthodoxy that defines those who doubt Francis) are said to number about a dozen, and what exercises them is the fear of a schism created by the pope. It is also an omen that in the late months of 2016 a theological study on the possibility of deposing a pope was reported to be making the rounds of the Vatican.

Those who are shocked to hear Francis described as a dictator would not question the fact that he is the most politically minded pope to come to the throne for many centuries. This characterization is not a libel of his enemies but is emphasized by so unqualified an admirer as Austen Ivereigh. We need to understand that the key to Francis's reckless style—the indifference to reform, the tyrannical acts, the feverish quest for popular approval—is that his prime concern is not in fact the government of the Church. Ivereigh has traced in detail Francis's ambition to make himself a political world leader; he set out with a bombastic vision of the "decadence" of Europe which would be exploited by Latin America to reassert itself, and his dream was to rally the continent into *"la patria grande"* (the great fatherland) to challenge the imperialist dominance of the United States. This objective was behind his appointment as secretary of state of Cardinal Parolin, who had been a much-praised papal nuncio to Mexico and Venezuela, and he was set to work to bind the continent together under the aegis of the Holy See. The actual results have been analysed by an Italian journalist:

> The image of Francis, who had chances to establish himself as "moral leader of the continent" ... is rapidly going into crisis, despite the outstanding work

of the Secretary of State Parolin: in Cuba…Vatican diplomacy is stumbling; in Colombia the peace referendum was lost ruinously because the country's Protestants sabotaged it; in Venezuela all political sides agree that the Vatican's peace-making effort has worsened rather than improved the situation; and finally in Brazil, after the success of the world youth day, Rio de Janeiro has a mayor who is a Protestant bishop, anti-Catholic, and above all critical of the Episcopal Conference.[27]

The election of Donald Trump shattered the assumptions on which Francis's political strategy was based. With all its macho Latin American rhetoric, the plan depended on the presence in the White House of a liberal president willing to abase himself (or herself) to Latin American claims. It collapses before a president whose response to troublemakers beyond the Rio Grande is to build a wall against them. That is why in 2016 Pope Francis staked all his chips on a Clinton presidency. Those around him, beginning with Cardinal Parolin, told him that Donald Trump had no hope of winning, and on Francis's orders the Administration of the Patrimony of the Apostolic See helped finance Hillary Clinton's presidential campaign. (It is now being said that the money used for it came from Peter's Pence, the donations of the faithful made supposedly for charitable purposes.)[28] Francis also intervened in the campaign by word, implicitly accusing Trump of not being a Christian. When Trump won, Francis was furious with his advisors. This may be one reason why Cardinal Parolin has lost favor: he proved himself fallible on predicting political outcomes in the United States, and he has failed to deliver the goods in Latin America.

The global scene in which Francis had pictured his triumph has changed out of recognition. With the rapprochement between the United States and Russia, and with Britain leaving the European Union, Germany and France are left huddled together, trying to protect the tatters of the liberal world order, an order in which Francis had wished to cast himself as the high priest. He now faces what is, for him, a political fiasco.

The White House has strong cards to play against the Vatican, and one may be surprised that it has so far held back from playing them. It is known that the CIA was monitoring the Conclave of 2013, and the thought that the American government might make use of its knowledge is said to be causing sleepless nights in the Curia. With the failure of the Holy See to reform its criminal financial structures, for which the evidence mounts day by day, one can readily imagine international financial bodies, led by America, deciding that enough is enough. The brutal dismissal in June 2017 of Libero Milone, the Vatican's auditor general, who is not without friends in America, might prove the final provocation.

The fundamental reason for this predicament is that Francis has gone beyond his limits. He is a clever politician—the cleverest to occupy the papal throne for centuries, well able to run rings round unsuspecting churchmen like Cardinals Burke, Sarah, and Müller—but as a world statesman he is out of his league. And while he may be a gifted politician within his limits, the Catholic Church requires higher talents than those of a Peronist party boss. More observers are becoming aware of this fact. Italian Luigi Bisignani wrote in the summer of 2017 that:

> After riding a press campaign that made an idol of the Argentinian Pope, people are realising that, essentially, Ratzinger's work has been profoundly underestimated. In a Vatican that was riven by feuds, the German Pope . . . [reformed the Vatican Bank], imposed zero tolerance on child abuse, and set out an in-depth study of the critical areas of the modern Church in the face of future challenges. Thus, Francis arrived with an unprecedented advantage of which perhaps even he was not aware, surrounded as he was by a mediocre clique who obscured his vision and who do not show him the danger points which risk assuming ever larger dimensions, distancing him also from his own predecessors.[29]

In 2016, the Vaticanist Giuseppe Nardi wrote: "Three-and-a-half years after the start of his pontificate, Pope Francis is reaching his limits. The impression, given by means of gestures and words, of a latent intention to change the doctrine of the Church must at some point either take on definite form or else it must collapse ... Francis finds himself cornered by means of the very atmosphere he himself is responsible for creating. It's no longer about a spontaneous utterance on this or that, which remains improvised and non-binding. His pastoral work and his leadership skills, which demand a sense of responsibility and an exemplary character, are reaching their limits. This could cause Francis to fail."[30]

Such comments point to the enormous blunder made by the Conclave in 2013 in choosing the cardinal "from the ends of the Earth" to be head of the Church. By voting for a little-known outsider, they elected a man who has proved unfit, by his character and by the priorities he shows, to hold his office. To many Catholics, this idea is difficult to take in. In living memory, we find no case in which such an error of judgment in the election of a pope has occurred. Some of the modern popes have been great men, others have been adequate; for centuries there has been none who was, as one must say brutally of Francis, so plainly beneath his office. How did it happen?

We should bear in mind that Jorge Bergoglio is a man brought up in a debased political culture, and trained in a religious order whose traditions of obedience and of political and social involvement were disrupted and distorted by the upheaval of the 1960s. This means that he was less formed in the long-rooted cultural disciplines that kept his predecessors up to certain standards. The Church has never been a stranger to clergy, even those of high character, who have let their religious vocation take too political a slant, and Bergoglio never showed the purity of dedication that would protect against such an error. Before his election, he did not distinguish himself by any of the spiritual or doctrinal writings or preachings for which many popes were known. His lack of interest in doctrine and liturgy is familiar, and even some of his habits of prayer have excited remark. Professor Lucrecia Rego de Planas commented that when celebrating Mass Pope Francis never genuflects to the tabernacle or the consecrated Host as liturgical rule prescribes, and he was known for that omission long before old age made it physically pardonable.[31] What are

Catholics to make of a pope who omits the signs of reverence to the Blessed Sacrament that all priests and faithful give by rule and by tradition?

We may link these defects to the low tone of the folksy magisterium that Pope Francis has made his trademark, in press conferences on international flights and other improvised alternatives to the Petrine cathedra. Italian journalist Aldo Maria Valli has pointed out "banalization as the dominant note and conformism as an intellectual habit"[32] of Pope Francis's pronouncements. One might say the same of the contorted insults that Pope Francis is famous for directing against those he rebukes, a phenomenon extended to his official documents. An encyclical such as *Evangelii gaudium* (2013) is full of phrases such as "narcissistic and authoritarian elitism," or "self-absorbed Promethean Neo-Pelagianism." Jesus Christ denounced "false prophets, who come to you in the clothing of sheep, but inwardly they are ravening wolves;" but we have had to wait till the pontificate of Francis to be warned, in papal teaching, of the dangers of sharing a pew with a Promethean Neo-Pelagian. This, apparently, is the language of a fresh new evangelization, inspired by the pastoral needs of the poor.

All this for a long time escaped the superficial gaze of the media, which is out of its depth in theology and falls for publicity gestures with childish naïveté. In Italy a number of journalists, of whom Sandro Magister stands out, have been reporting critically on Vatican affairs for some years, but in the English-speaking world the silence has been deafening. Only a handful of conservative Catholic websites, including the *National Catholic Register* and LifeSiteNews, have been producing, for doctrinal reasons, the kind of sharp reporting that the mainstream media have been neglecting. Italy has also produced two critical books, Antonio Socci's *Non è Francesco* (2014) and Aldo Maria Valli's *266.* (2016). In America signs are beginning to appear of a breaking of ranks, at least in the publishing world: George Neumayr's *The Political Pope* (2017) presents the conservative case against Francis, and it has been followed by Philip Lawler's *Lost Shepherd: How Pope Francis Is Misleading His Flock* (2018).

In recent months the signs have been mounting that "you cannot fool all the people all the time." The media consensus hailing Francis as a great reformer showed a serious crack on July 2, 2017, when the Roman daily *Il Tempo* devoted its front page and pages two and three to a series of articles assessing his achievements and finding them wanting. The central article was under the headline, *"Crollo di fedeli, temi etici, gay, immigrati e Isis-Islam. Quanti errori. Ora le epurazioni. Cala la popolarità di Francesco."* ("Drop in faithful, ethical issues, gays, immigrants and Isis-Islam. How many mistakes! Now the purges. Francis's popularity stalls.") The rapid departure from the Vatican of Libero Milone, Cardinal Müller, and Cardinal Pell could not fail to suggest a state of crisis, and the attempt to explain it in terms of Pope Francis shedding his wrong choices is bound to succumb before more probing enquiry. If indeed, money from Peter's Pence was diverted to fund Hillary Clinton's presidential campaign, at Pope Francis's request, as has been repeatedly rumored from reliable sources, it could be the unraveling of an enormous scandal.

Pope Francis still has one overwhelming advantage. The liberal media have invested heavily in him as a revolutionary idol—the man whom the *Wall Street Journal* in December 2016 described as the "leader of the global left"—and they are not ready to give up the myth. With Obama gone and Hillary Clinton humiliated, Francis is more necessary to them than ever. To non-Christians, the concerns that Francis is stirring by his attempts to liberalize sexual moral teaching are irrelevant. Indeed, what the secularists love about Francis is the way his tradition-breaking style undermines the mystique and the authority of the Church. Yet the belief that the liberal media can impose their view on the world has recently taken a knocking. Hillary Clinton relied on them, and failed; we might see Pope Francis go the same way.

Finally, it is worth commenting on the book you hold in your hands. An earlier Italian version, *Il Papa Dittatore*, was published in electronic form on November 21, 2017, and the reaction from the Vatican gave a new illustration of the pope's concern for his image and his habit of tight control. In the first few days, the Vatican thought that it had identified a gentleman living in England as the pseudonymous author, and he began to receive harassing telephone calls. When this proved a false cast, the search spread further, and on December 12 a Vatican journalist passed on to me a report that a short list of six possible authors had been laid before the pope. No less revealing was the speech that Pope Francis made on December 21 on occasion of the presentation of Christmas greetings by the Curia, a gathering by now familiar as the scene for nagging rebukes by the pontiff.[33] Reacting to the allegations that his pontificate was barren in reforms, Francis recited a list of changes that had been made (though these did nothing to address the specific criticisms in this book). His speech further attacked "betrayers of trust and exploiters of the Church's

motherhood"—which might be an allusion to the disclosures by
Vatican sources without which the recent exposé would not have
been possible. But there was a misrepresentation from an opposite quarter with which Pope Francis also took issue, the one
which, for example, represents him as an unworldly old recluse
who only reads one newspaper and has not watched television
for twenty years. The pope took occasion to disparage the view
that he was ill-informed. Thus, a last-ditch defense of Pope Francis, which we are hearing nowadays, that his reforming intentions are being frustrated by an obfuscating staff, is discarded
by its beneficiary. Indeed, nobody in touch with the Casa Santa
Marta would doubt that Francis's speciality is a minute control
of what goes on in the Vatican and beyond. What is increasingly
in question is his judgment and his capacity to continue project-
ing the image that has served him so well until now.

In the early months of 2018, two signs appeared that Francis
is likely to be overtaken by the wide-ranging corruption in which
he has made himself personally complicit. One was the revelation
of the scandalous state in the diocese of his right-hand man,
Cardinal Rodríguez Maradiaga, in Honduras—a network of
abuses whose details are gradually coming out, despite the pope's
efforts to hush them up.[34] The other relates to a scandal which
already has a lurid history in Italy, that of the Istituto Dermo-
patico dell'Immacolata (IDI). This dermatological hospital in
Rome has been accused of malpractices on a huge scale, including
money-laundering and tax fraud. In 2016 the Italian finance
police discovered that the hospital had colossal liabilities, which
included a debt of 845 million euros and an imputed sum of 450
million in tax evasion, while eighty-two million had been diverted

and six million euros of public funds embezzled. The involvement of Cardinal Giuseppe Versaldi, who in 2015 was edged aside from the presidency of the Prefecture of Economic Affairs after he tried to conceal from the pope that thirty million euros had been diverted from the Bambino Gesù hospital to IDI, has already been mentioned.[35] In 2017 the vast debts of IDI caught up with the Vatican in a situation of critical urgency, compelling recourse to the Papal Foundation in the USA, an organization of rich donors who commit themselves to making grants to the Holy See for the relief of poverty.

In the summer of 2017, Pope Francis, in a personal intervention, appealed to the Foundation for a grant of twenty-five million dollars to be used as a tide-over loan to IDI. A grant of eight million dollars was accordingly voted through in December by the bishops on the board, against lay opposition, and in January 2018, despite alarms raised by the Foundation's lay members, a further five-million-dollar vote was forced through by the board's chairman, Cardinal Donald Wuerl. These unprecedented grants were not only novel in their destination but were in the order of a hundred times greater than those customarily made by the Foundation, which seldom exceed 200,000 dollars at a time. The decision prompted the resignation of the head of the Papal Foundation's audit committee, who reported: "I found this grant to be negligent in character, and contrary to the spirit of the Foundation.... Instead of helping the poor in a third-world country, the board approved an unprecedented huge grant to a hospital that has a history of mismanagement, criminal indictments, and bankruptcy."[36] The intervention exposed the irony of Pope Francis's program of "the Church of the poor," which is not only shown as dependent on the generosity of multi-millionaire American donors but is liable to diversion, as needs require, to cover up mind-boggling financial corruption on the Vatican's home ground.

The Next Pope

We come back to the unprecedented blunder committed by the cardinals in 2013 in electing such a man as Jorge Bergoglio. Catholics are accustomed to the election of a pope being praiseworthy, or at least adequate, and they will find it difficult to believe (even with a clique of scheming cardinals to explain it) that such a literally unholy error could have been made. Yet no election procedure is immune against mistakes, however rare the experience may be. One has to go back quite a few centuries to find popes who have been outright personal disasters, but it has happened, as one might expect.

Probably the last pope with such a worldly and political approach as Francis's was Urban VIII (1623–1644). He involved the papacy in a disastrous war with neighboring principalities, and at Urban's death the Holy See was bankrupt and his family was chased out of Rome. The more lasting damage that Urban did to the Church was his condemnation of Galileo, not because he considered that the astronomical theory of heliocentricity was heretical (the erroneous view that is often taken of the incident) but in personal revenge for the apparent insult to the pope that Galileo had woven into his book on the subject.

Perhaps a closer parallel was a ruler such as Paul IV (1555–1559), a zealot for religious poverty who was elected pope in his seventies. His political obsessions led him to fight against the

Emperor Charles V, the prime champion of the Catholic cause in the war against Protestantism that was raging at that time, and he quarreled, again for political reasons, with Mary Tudor and Cardinal Pole, who were engaged in the difficult task of restoring Catholicism in England. His reign ended in political scandal and popular riots against him. Or one might consider Urban VI (1378–1389), who was elected as a complete outsider and soon showed that he lacked the mental balance for his office. The cardinals asked him to abdicate, and on his refusal declared him deposed and elected an antipope, thus initiating the forty-year Western Schism. Urban responded by creating a job lot of twenty-nine cardinals to replace those who had deserted him, but he soon quarreled with these too and executed five of them for plotting against him, while several others went over to the rival side.

Cases such as these illustrate the dangers of placing a loose cannon aboard St. Peter's Bark, and the difficulty of deposing a pope.[37] Whether such a deposition happens, or whether we await God's more usual way of causing a vacancy in the Apostolic See, the great question will be what happens in the election of the next pope, and there is no certainty that the same mistake will not be made again. Let us note that the cardinals who are said to be moving against Pope Francis are precisely the Curial set who, in 2013, decided to put their weight behind Bergoglio and thus ensured his election. This time round, the candidate they are putting forward is Cardinal Parolin. One sincerely hopes that the Sacred College has learned a better lesson.

We may reflect that even the cardinals who have been created by Pope Francis during his pontificate—reportedly in a deliberate attempt to pack the next Conclave—do not necessarily share

Francis's view of the Church as a political instrument. Let us appeal to them, and pray to God, that they may reject the disastrous vision that has brought the Church to confusion and revert to a spiritual model of what a pope ought to be.

Let us pray that the participants in the next Conclave ensure that no clique can turn the election to its own agenda, and that they know well whom they are electing. Let him be a man of established repute in the Church, and above all known as a man of God and not a politician; a man whose priorities are the spiritual treasures he is called to guard; a man who teaches doctrine openly and not in ambiguous backroom deals; a man who will be a sincere reformer and will not ally himself with the corrupt in a bid to control the Church. It is for the cardinals to do the right thing in their consciences and leave the rest in the hands of God. And let us pray that, in following their consciences, the cardinals might never again place a dictator pope in the See of St. Peter.

NOTES

Chapter 1: The St. Gallen Mafia

1. Jeanne Smits, "Cardinal Danneels Admits Being Part of Clerical 'Mafia' that plotted Francis' election," LifeSiteNews, September 25, 2015, https://www.lifesitenews.com/news/cardinal-danneels-admits-being-part-of-clerical-mafia-that-plotted-francis.

2. "Geheime Papstwahl in St. Gallen" ("Secret Papal Election in St. Gallen"), Report in FM1 Today, September 29, 2015, http://www.fm1today.ch/geheime-papstwahl-in-st-gallen/36070.

3. Edward Pentin, "Cardinal Danneels Admits to Being Part of 'Mafia' Club Opposed to Benedict XVI," *National Catholic Register*, Septermber 24, 2015, http://www.ncregister.com/blog/edward-pentin/cardinal-danneels-part-of-mafia-club-opposed-to-benedict-xvi; Edward Pentin, "Cardinal Danneels' Biographers Retract Comments on St. Gallen Group," *National Catholic Register*, September 26, 2015, http://m.ncregister.com/46711/b#.WnnVqbYrIzU.

4. Maike Hickson, "The Themes of the Synod, the Themes of the Sankt Gallen 'Mafia club,'" LifeSiteNews, October 24, 2015, https://www.lifesitenews.com/opinion/the-themes-of-the-synod-the-themes-of-the-sankt-gallen-mafia-club.

5. Anian Christoph Wimmer, "Was Paul Badde über die Gruppe 'Sankt Gallen' wusste—Und: Wer die Synode entscheidet" ("What Paul Badde knew about the 'St Gallen' Group—And: Who decides the Synod"), Catholic News Agency, October 10, 2015, http://de.catholicnewsagency.com/story/was-paul-badde-uber-die-gruppe-sankt-gallen-wusste-und-wer-die-synode-entscheidet-0085.

6. http://www.bistum-stgallen.ch/download_temp/Erkl%E4rung%20em.%20Bischof%20Ivo%20F%FCrer.pdf.

7. Edward Pentin, "Cardinal Danneels' Biographers Retract Comments on St. Gallen Group: But the Cardinal's Assertion That the Secretive 'Mafia-Like' Group Existed and Opposed Joseph Ratzinger Still Stands," National Catholic Register, September 26, 2015, http://www.ncregister.com/blog/edward-pentin/st.-gallen-group-not-a-lobby-group-say-authors.

8. See chapter four.

9. Sandro Magister, "Il Gesù del cardinale Martini non avrebbe mai scritto la 'Humanae Vitae'" ("Cardinal Martini's Jesus Would Never Have Written 'Humanae Vitae'"), Chiesa Espresso, November 3, 2008, http://chiesa.espresso.repubblica.it/articolo/209045bdc4.html?eng=y.

10. Titled, "Due in una carne. Chiesa e sessualità nella storia" ("Two in one flesh: Church and sexuality in history"). Magister writes: "The two authors were both militant feminists during the 1970's and are both historians, one of them secularist, the other Catholic: Margherita Pelaja and Lucetta Scaraffia."

11. On June 14, 2017 Vaticanist Roberto de Mattei confirmed the rumors that Pope Francis intends to set up a "secret" commission to "reinterpret" the teaching in *Humanae vitae* "in the light of" his post-synodal apostolic exhortation, *Amoris laetitia*. Monsignor Gilfredo Marengo, Professor at John Paul II Pontifical Institute, is to be its head. Marengo has decried the view that the Catholic faith is "impermeable to questions and provocations of the here and now," [*impermeabile alle domande e alle provocazioni del qui e ora*]and commented during the Synods on the Family that, in the past, the Church has "presented a too abstract theological ideal on marriage, almost artificially constructed, far from the concrete situation and the effective possibilities of families as they really are." Roberto de Mattei, "De Mattei: The Plan of 'Reinterpretation' for Humanae Vitae," Rorate Caeli blog, June 14, 2017, https://rorate-caeli.blogspot.com/2017/06/de-mattei-plan-of-reinterpretation-for.html.

12. Interview by Fr. Georg Sporschill, SJ, in *Corriere della Sera*, September 1, 2012, "L'addio a Martini: Chiesa indietro di 200 anni," http://www.corriere.it/cronache/12_settembre_02/le-parole-ultima-intervista_cdb2993e-f50b-11e1-9f30-3ee01883d8dd.shtml.

13. Pope Francis, "Angelus," The Holy See website, March 17, 2013, https://w2.vatican.va/content/francesco/en/angelus/2013/documents/papa-francesco_angelus_20130317.html.

14. David Gibson, "Cardinal Kasper, the 'Pope's Theologian,' Downplays Vatican Blast at U.S. Nuns," *National Catholic Reporter*, May 6, 2014, https://www.ncronline.org/news/vatican/cardinal-kasper-popes-theologian-downplays-vatican-blast-us-nuns.

15. Matthew Boudway and Grant Gallicho, "An Interview with Cardinal Walter Kasper," *Commonweal*, May 7, 2014, https://www.commonwealmagazine.org/interview-cardinal-walter-kasper.

16. Gian Guido Vecchi, "Il teologo riformista Kasper: 'Gay si nasce, no ai fondamentalisti in nome del Vangelo,'" *Corriere della Sera*, October 1, 2015, http://roma.corriere.it/notizie/cronaca/15_ottobre_01/teologo-riformista-kasper-gay-si-nasce-no-fondamentalisti-nome-vangelo-28db8158-6800-11e5-8caa-10c7357f56e4.shtml; Thomas D. Williams, "Cardinal Kasper Gears Up for Vatican Synod: 'You Are Born Gay,'" Breitbart, October 2, 2015, http://www.breitbart.com/national-security/2015/10/02/cardinal-kasper-gears-vatican-synod-born-gay/.

17. See Hilary White, "Gay 'Marriage' a 'Positive Development': Retired Belgian Cardinal Danneels," LifeSiteNews, June 5, 2013, https://www.lifesitenews.com/news/gay-marriage-a-positive-development-retired-belgian-cardinal-danneels.

18. Hilary White, "Cardinal Danneels Urged Sex Abuse Victim to Silence: Secret Recordings," LifeSiteNews, August 30, 2010, https://www.lifesitenews.com/news/cardinal-danneels-urged-sex-abuse-victim-to-silence-secret-recordings.

19. Steven Erlanger, "Belgian Church Leader Urged Victim to Be Silent," *New York Times*, August 29, 2010, http://www.nytimes.com/2010/08/30/world/europe/30belgium.html.

20. Colin Randall, "Police Raid Home of Belgian Archbishop in Sex Abuse Probe," *Daily Mail*, June 25, 2010, http://www.dailymail.co.uk/news/article-1289283/Police-raid-home-Belgian-archbishop-sex-abuse-probe.html.

21. Lucio Brunelli, "Così eleggemmo papa Ratzinger," *Limes*, August 31, 2009, http://www.limesonline.com/cosi-eleggemmo-papa-ratzinger/5959.

22. Miguel Cullen, "Pope Sent Greetings to the Queen Straight after His Election, Says Cardinal," *Catholic Herald*, September 12, 2013, http://www.catholicherald.co.uk/news/2013/09/12/pope-sent-greeting-to-queen-straight-after-his-election-says-cardinal/.

23. Ibid.

24. Paul Vallely, "Pope Francis Puts People First and Dogma Second. Is This Really the New Face of Catholicism?" *Independent*, July 31, 2013, http://www.independent.co.uk/voices/comment/pope-francis-puts-people-first-and-dogma-second-is-this-really-the-new-face-of-catholicism-8740242.html.

25. Andrea Tornielli, "Tentazione sudamericana per il primo Papa extraeuropeo," *La Stampa*, March 2, 2013, http://www.lastampa.it/2013/03/02/italia/cronache/tentazione-sudamericana-per-il-primo-papa-extraeuropeo-XvX5JzVJsZR6Sf99SmPAQJ/pagina.html?zanpid=2310082555195880448.

26. Matthew Schmitz, "Burying Benedict," *First Things*, May 22, 2017, https://www.firstthings.com/web-exclusives/2017/05/burying-benedict.

Chapter 2: The Cardinal from Argentina

1. Omar Bello, *El Verdadero Francisco* (Buenos Aires: 2013), 60.

2. Austen Ivereigh, *The Great Reformer* (New York: 2014), 67, 78.

3. Bello, *El Verdadero Francisco*, 13.

4. See Ivereigh, *The Great Reformer*, 103, 106.

5. Emilio Mignone, *Iglesia y Dictadura: el papel de la Iglesia a la luz de sus relaciones con el régimen militar* (Buenos Aires: 1986).

6. Sergio Rubin and Francesca Ambrogetti, *El Jesuita* (Buenos Aires: 2010).

7. Bello, *El Verdadero Francisco*, 75.

8. Omar Bello tells this story without naming the subject, and asserts that he was dismissed because of an indiscretion over Bergoglio's biography *El Jesuita* (see *El Verdadero Francisco*, 36–37). This appears to be incorrect; the real motive for the archbishop's displeasure is uncertain.

9. Bello, *El Verdadero Francisco*, 34.

10. See "Carta al Papa Francisco por Lucrecia Rego de Planas," Stat Veritas blog, September 27, 2013, statveritasblog.blogspot. it/2013/09/carta-al-papa-francisco-por-lucrecia.html.

11. *"Desconfiado como una vaca tuerta."* Bello, *El Verdadero Francisco*, 181 and see 196 for the next quotation.

12. Ivereigh, *The Great Reformer*, 252.

13. On this episode see also below, pages 159–60.

14. Ivereigh, *The Great Reformer*, 264.

15. Antonio Caponnetto, *La Iglesia Traicionada* (Buenos Aires: 2010), 120–21.

16. Ivereigh, *The Great Reformer*, 243–44.

17. See Francisco José de La Cigoña, "Los peones de Bergoglio," in the Spanish newspaper *Intereconomía*, December 26, 2011.

18. Ibid.

19. Bello, *El Verdadero Francisco*, 29.

20. Information from private sources in Buenos Aires.

21. Bello, *El Verdadero Francisco*, 32. A good laugh awaits those who care to compare these details with the saintly account given by Austen Ivereigh, *The Great Reformer*, 350–51.

22. Cardinal McCarrick revealed this in a public talk on October 1, 2013. See Pete Baklinski, "They Gave Pope Francis Four Years to 'Make the Church over Again,'" LifeSiteNews, October 1, 2013.

23. Antonio Socci, *Non è Francesco* (Milan: 2014). The fact that a fifth ballot was held is well known; see e.g., Ivereigh, *The Great Reformer*, 361.

Chapter 3: Reform? What Reform?

1. Lucrecia Rego de Planas, *Carta al Papa Francisco*, September 23, 2013. See note 10 to chapter two.

2. See H.J.A. Sire, *Phoenix from the Ashes* (Ohio: 2015), 370 etc., which gives an account of the historical background.

3. Damian Thompson, "Why More and More Priests Can't Stand Pope Francis," *Spectator*, January 14, 2017.

4. Gianluigi Nuzzi, *Merchants in the Temple* (2015), 198–99.

5. Aldo Maria Valls, *266* (Macerata: 2016), 106. The cryptic title of this book is Francis's number in the list of popes.

6. Ibid., 107.

7. Quoted in an article in NDTV, June 11, 2013: "Pope Francis Admits to 'Gay Lobby' in Vatican Administration: Report."

8. One cardinal reports that on the eve of the Conclave Rodríguez Maradiaga was busy in the Honduran embassy telephoning potential floating voters, including Cardinals Pell, Ouellet, O'Malley, and Hummes, to solicit their vote for Bergoglio.

9. Emiliano Fittipaldi, "Il cardinale da 35 mila euro al mese: in Vaticano scoppia un nuovo scandalo," *L'Espresso*, December 21, 2017; Edward Pentin, "Cardinal Maradiaga Denies Financial Allegations, But Questions Remain Unanswered," *National Catholic Register*, December 23, 2017; Damian

Thompson, "Time Is Running Out for the "Dictator Pope" as a New Scandal Hits Rome," *The Spectator*, December 23, 2017.

10. Gianluigi Nuzzi, *Merchants in the Temple* (2015), 153.

11. Marco Tosatti, "Waiting for Vatican Reform," *First Things*, June 6, 2017, from which the details of the next three paragraphs are taken.

12. These events were described in full by Sandro Magister in the article "Il prelato del lobby gay" in *L'Espresso*, June 18, 2013.

13. Francesco Antonio Grana, "Vaticano, fermato un monsignore: festini gay e droga al Palazzo dell' ex Sant' Uffizio," *Il Fatto Quotidiano*, June 28, 2017.

14. Matthew Cullinam Hoffman, "Vatican Archbishop Featured in Homoerotic Painting He Commissioned," LifeSiteNews, March 3, 2017, https://www.lifesitenews.com/news/leading-vatican-archbishop-featured-in-homoerotic-painting-he-commissioned.

15. In a statement, read by Archbishop Silvano Maria Tomasi at the UN Human Rights Council on September 22, 2009, the Holy See stated that the majority of Catholic clergy who had committed acts of sexual abuse should not be viewed as pedophiles, but as homosexuals who are attracted to sex with adolescent males. The statement said that rather than pedophilia, "it would be more correct to speak of ephebophilia; being a homosexual attraction to adolescent males…Of all priests involved in the abuses, 80 to 90% belong to this sexual orientation minority which is sexually engaged with adolescent boys between the ages of 11 and 17."

16. Peter Tatchell, the UK's highest-profile homosexualist campaigner, was among the most vocal critics of the Catholic "priest paedophiles." In 2010 he was among those who opposed the visit of Pope Benedict XVI to Britain, accusing him of having

covered for the abusers. The same year, Tatchell, who has written that "not all sex involving children is unwanted, abusive and harmful," was advocating lowering the legal age of consent to allow adult men to engage in homosexual activity with fourteen-year-olds.

17. "Instruction Concerning the Criteria for the Discernment of Vocations with regard to Persons with Homosexual Tendencies in view of their Admission to the Seminary and to Holy Orders" Congregation for Catholic Education, approved by Pope Benedict, August 31, 2005.

18. The 'Motu Proprio' Sacramentorum Sanctitatis Tutela was a restatement of the Apostolic Constitution on the Roman Curia, Regimini Ecclesiae Universae, by Paul VI, issued in 1967, that "confirmed the [CDF] Congregation's judicial and administrative competence in proceeding 'according to its amended and approved norms.'"

19. "Pope Has 'Cleaned Up Episcopate,' Nuncio Says," EWTN, February 22, 2013, http://www.ewtnnews.com/catholic-news/World.php?id=7089.

20. "Argentina Probes Sex Abuse at Deaf School, What Vatican Knew," Crux, December 24, 2016, https://cruxnow.com/global-church/2016/12/24/argentina-probes-sex-abuse-deaf-school-what-vatican-knew/.

21. Nicole Winfield, "Pope Quietly Trims Sanctions for Sex Abusers Seeking Mercy," Associated Press, February 25, 2017, https://apnews.com/64e1fc2312764a24bf1b2d6ec3bf4caf/pope-quietly-trims-sanctions-sex-abusers-seeking-mercy.

22. Pinto's name is on the famous "Lista Pecorelli," a list of alleged Freemasons within the Church compiled in the 1970s by Carmine "Mino" Pecorelli, director of *L'Osservatorio Politico*, a press agency specializing in political scandals and crimes. The

Lista Pecorelli was published in *Osservatorio Politico Internazionale* magazine, September 12, 1978, during the brief pontificate of Pope John Paul I.

23. Michael Brendan Dougherty, "A Child Abuse Scandal Is Coming for Pope Francis," in *Week,* January 3, 2017.

24. "Sex Abuse at Deaf School," Crux.

25. "Francis's Commitment to Abuse Survivors in Question," *National Catholic Reporter,* January 23, 2018.

26. Inés San Martín, "Mixed Verdicts for Ex-Vatican Official in Corruption Trial," Crux, January 19, 2016.

27. John L. Allen "Arrested Monsignor Charges Corruption in Vatican Finances," *National Catholic Register,* October 3, 2013.

28. Gianluigi Nuzzi, *Merchants in the Temple,* 76.

29. Nuzzi, *Merchants in the Temple,* 56.

30. Nuzzi, *Merchants in the Temple,* 202.

31. Nuzzi, *Merchants in the Temple*, 113. Linguists may be interested to note that *calcagno* is the Italian for "heel."

32. Francesco Peloso, "Vaticano, la guerra tra dicasteri finanziari frena la riforma del papa," *Lettera 43*, May 21, 2017. Peloso writes: *"Alla guida dell' APSA è rimasto il cardinale Calcagno, indagato per attivitá immobiliari che avrebbero finito per danneggiare le stesse casse della diocesi. Eppure è ancora al suo posto."* (At the head of APSA remains Cardinal Calcagno, who is under investigation for real-estate dealings which ended by harming the funds of his own diocese. And yet he is still in office.)

33. Nina Fabrizio and Fausto Gasparroni, "Crac Divina Provvidenza: spunta cardinale Versaldi: 'Tacere al Papa 30 milioni sull Idi.'" Agenzia Nazionale Stampa Associata, June 20, 2015. This type of malversation was not new: two years earlier four hundred thousand

euros had been diverted from the funds of the Bambino Gesù to refurbish the apartment of Cardinal Bertone, the then secretary of state. (See below, note 38.)

34. Nuzzi, *Merchants in the Temple*, 81.
35. Nuzzi, *Merchants in the Temple*, 53–54, 169–70.
36. This interpretation is supported by the article in *World Economy,* November 4, 2015: Reuters, "Vatican Inspectors Suspect Key Office Used for Money Laundering."
37. Franca Giansoldati, "Vaticano, scandalo case: un buco di 700 mila euro," *Il Messaggero*, April 29, 2016.
38. In July 2017 an exception belatedly came along when the Vatican's court began to try the relatively minor case of the four hundred thousand euros that were diverted from the funds of the Bambino Gesù hospital to refurbish Cardinal Bertone's apartment. (See above, note 33.) Significantly, the trigger for this prosecution may have been the irritation of Pope Francis at the fact that Cardinal Bertone has exercised his right to continue living in the Vatican even after his dismissal as secretary of state.
39. Philip Lawler, "The drive for Vatican reform has stalled," *Catholic Culture*, April 21, 2016.
40. Philip Lawler, "Another Blow to Vatican Transparency and Accountability," LifeSiteNews, July 11, 2016.
41. Francis X. Rocca, "The Trials and Tribulations of the Vatican's Financial Chief: Pope Francis Trimmed Powers of Cardinal George Pell, Charged with Cleaning Up the City-State's Muddled Accounts, in Setback for Broader Overhaul of Vatican," *Wall Street Journal,* September 7, 2016.
42. John Allen, Crux, December 8, 2016.
43. Carl Olson, "Is Cardinal Pell 'the Quintessential Scapegoat'?" *Catholic World Report*, July 13, 2017. It is worth noting that

much of the unpopularity that Cardinal Pell garnered in Australia was from the homosexual lobby, who resented the stand he took in that connection.

44. Francesco Peloso, "Vaticano, la guerra tra dicasteri finanziari frena la riforma del papa," *Lettera 43*, May 21, 2017; Edward Pentin, "Cardinal Pell Reprimands Vatican's Real Estate Body for Exceeding Its Authority," *National Catholic Register*, May 10, 2017.

45. Philip Lawler, "The Vatican Auditor Resigns—Another Crushing Blow for Financial Reform," *Catholic Culture*, June 20, 2017.

46. Interview by Libero Milone given to *Corriere della Sera, Wall Street Journal,* Reuters and *Sky Tg24*, published by *Corriere della Sera* September 24, 2017. See also the article by Philip Pullella in Reuters World News of the same date: "Auditor says he was forced to quit Vatican after finding irregularities."

47. For details of this, see below, chapter six.

48. Fiorenza Sarzanini, "Licenziato il numero due dello Ior «Scortato fuori del Vaticano»," *Corriere della Sera*, November 29, 2017.

Chapter 4: Beating a New (Crooked) Path

1. Gerhard Ludwig Cardinal Müller, *Testimony to the Power of Grace: On the Indissolubility of Marriage and the Debate Concerning Civilly Remarried and the Sacrament*, vatican.va, October 23, 2014.

2. "The Synod on the Family, Kasper and the Call for Mercy," *Rorate Caeli*, February 26, 2014.

3. Marco Tosatti, *La Stampa*, March 24, 2014. Quoted in English in "Very Relevant: Exclusive for La Stampa," *Rorate Caeli*, March 26, 2014.

4. Cardinal Walter Kasper, *The Gospel of the Family* (New York: 2014), 43.

5. Junno Arocho Esteves, "Fr Lombardi: Consistory Focused on Pastoral Vision of the Family," *Zenit*, February 20, 2014.

6. "Pope Francis Expresses Support for Cardinal Kasper's 'Serene Theology' on the Family," Rome Reports, February 21, 2014.

7. An overview of Cardinal Nichols's positions can be read at "Cardinal Who Supports LGBT Radicals Is Moderator of English-Speaking Synod Group," *Voice of the Family*, October 9, 2015.

8. Gerard O'Connell, "Murphy-O'Connor: Francis Is Open, Honest and Made People Feel Free", *Vatican Insider*, March 13, 2014.

9. "Cinq cardinaux rappellent leur ferme position doctrinale avant le Synode sur la famille," *La Croix*, September 17, 2014.

10. "Intervista al cardinale Kasper: «Vogliono la guerra al Sinodo, il Papa è il bersaglio»," *Il Mattino*, September 18, 2014.

11. John-Henry Westen, "You Should Come up Here if You Know Everything': Cardinal Fires Back as Press Questions Synod's 'Lack of Transparency,'" LifeSiteNews, October 3, 2014.

12. Zenit Staff, "Pope Francis' Homily at Opening Mass of Extraordinary Synod on the Family," Zenit, October 5, 2014.

13. John-Henry Westen and Hilary White, "Pope Francis Distances Himself from 'Very Conservative' Bishops," LifeSiteNews, October 8, 2014.

14. Edward Pentin, *The Rigging of a Vatican Synod? An Investigation into Alleged Manipulation at the Extraordinary Synod on the Family* (San Francisco: 2015), 51.

15. Ibid.

16. Associated Press, "Top Vatican Cardinal Wants Family Speeches Public," *Daily Mail*, October 9, 2014.

17. "Full Text of Cardinal Burke's Major Interview to Il Foglio on the Synod," *Rorate Caeli*, October 16, 2014.
18. Pentin, *Rigging of a Vatican Synod?*, 21.
19. Ibid., 37.
20. "Cardinal Pell: Synod Says No to Secular Agenda," *Catholic News Service*, October 16, 2014.
21. "Cardinal Burke to CWR: Confirms Transfer, Praises Pushback, Addresses Controversy over Remarks by Cardinal Kasper," *Catholic World Report*, October 18, 2014.
22. Pentin, *Rigging of a Vatican Synod?*, 150.
23. Ibid., 180.
24. Edward Pentin, "Statement on Cardinal Kasper Interview," October 16, 2014, Edward Pentin.
25. Pentin, *Rigging of a Vatican Synod?*, 130.
26. "Cardinal Burke to CWR," *Catholic World Report*.
27. "Pope Francis Speech at the Conclusion of the Synod," Vatican Radio, October 18, 2014.
28. Christa Pongratz-Lippit, "Cardinal Marx: Pope Francis Has Pushed open the Doors of the Church," *National Catholic Reporter*, October 28, 2014.
29. Pentin, *Rigging of a Vatican Synod?*, 61.
30. *Donum vitae*, Congregation for the Doctrine of the Faith, February 22, 1987; *Dignitas personae*, Congregation for the Doctrine of the Faith, September 8, 2008.
31. Allegedly, Dew, one of Francis's recent appointments to the College of Cardinals, was the bishop quoted by Father Rosica as saying that the Church should abandon its language of condemnation for sin. During the October 2005 Synod, Archbishop Dew argued for the admission of the divorced and remarried to Holy Communion.

32. Later identified as Pope Francis's main ghostwriter for *Amoris laetitia*.

33. Robert Cardinal Sarah, "What Sort of Pastoral Mercy in Response to New Challenges on the Family? A Reading of the *Lineamenta*," *Christ's New Homeland Africa: Contribution to the Synod by African Pastors* (San Francisco: 2015).

34. Sandro Magister, "Thirteen Cardinals Have Written to the Pope. Here's the Letter," Chiesa Espresso, October 12, 2015.

35. Mario Valenza, "Papa Bergoglio: scoppio d'ira e malore dopo la lettera dei cardinali," *Il Giornale*, October 13, 2015.

36. Edward Pentin, "Married Couples Have Their Say at the Synod," *National Catholic Register*, October 8, 2015.

37. "Has the Intervention of Pope Francis Returned the Synod to a Heterodox Trajectory?," *Voice of the Family*, October 7, 2017.

38. Ibid.

39. "Ceremony Commemorating the 50th Anniversary of the Institution of Synod of Bishops: Address of His Holiness Pope Francis," vatican.va, October 17, 2015.

40. "Papal Calls for Decentralization Put Integrity of Catholic Doctrine at Risk," Voice of the Family, October 22, 2015.

41. A detailed analysis of the *Relatio Synodi* of the Ordinary Synod can be found in "Analysis of the Final Report of the Ordinary Synod," Voice of the Family, March 10, 2016.

42. John Paul II, *Familiaris consortio*, No. 84.

43. "Bishop Athanasius Schneider on the Synod on the Family," LifeSiteNews, November 5, 2014.

44. "Buenos Aires Bishops' Guidelines on Amoris Laetitia: Full Text," Catholic Voices Comment, September 18, 2016.

45. Thus the previous requirement, that of living together "as brother and sister," has been relegated to a suggestion. Walter Kasper summarized the position in an interview with

Commonweal: "To live together as brother and sister? Of course I have high respect for those who are doing this. But it's a heroic act, and heroism is not for the average Christian."

46. The Maltese bishops' *"Criteria for the Application of Chapter VIII of Amoris Laetitia"* has drawn criticism from canon lawyers, and some Vatican officials who argued that it appeared to assert the primacy of conscience over the objective moral truth. It states that remarried divorcees can receive Communion after a period of discernment, with an informed and enlightened conscience, and if they are "at peace with God."

47. Andrea Tornielli, "Pope Francis on the Correct Interpretation of the "Amoris Laetitia," Vatican Insider, September 12, 2016.

48. Most of the signatory cardinals were retired; the only one of them who still held an official post was Cardinal Burke, who was patronus of the Order of Malta.

49. See below, page 178–79.

50. Jérôme Lejeune (d. 1994) was a devout Catholic geneticist and pediatrician and member of the Pontifical Academy of Sciences who discovered the genetic origin of Down syndrome and other genetic disorders. He spent the rest of his career campaigning against the use of this knowledge to target such babies for abortion. His cause for canonization has been formally opened.

51. Bishop Cardoso Sobrinho's clarification came in a letter which *L'Osservatore Romano*, controlled by Fisichella's friends in the Secretariat of State, refused to print.

52. The matter was finally resolved only after a complete dossier on the facts was sent directly to Pope Benedict XVI. CDF head Cardinal Levada issued a formal statement reiterating Catholic teaching in all its points on the sanctity of human life.

53. See above, page 64.

54. The new statutes stipulate that Ordinary Members are appointed "on the basis of their academic qualifications, proven professional integrity, professional expertise and faithful service in the defence and promotion of the right to life of every human person." The statutes' emphasis on the "magisterium of the Church" is less direct, saying only that its purpose is to "to form persons…with full respect for the Magisterium of the Church," but specifies that "Academicians are selected, without regard for their religion." "New Academicians commit themselves to promoting and defending the principles regarding the value of life and the dignity of the human person, *interpreted in a way consonant with* the Church's Magisterium." [Emphasis added.] The new statutes make no mention of any oath; instead a "declaration of the servants of life" to be signed by all new members is given in a separate document.

55. Jan Bentz, "Pope Francis Has Removed Every Single Member of the Vatican Pro-Life Academy," LifeSiteNews, February 17, 2017.

56. "Philosopher Who Backs Legal Abortion appointed to Vatican Pro-Life Academy," *Catholic Herald*, June 13, 2017.

57. The Pontifical Council for the Family was merged into the new Dicastery for Laity, Family, and Life in August 2016, headed by Bishop Kevin Farrell, who was also made a cardinal. Cardinal Farrell later chided Archbishop Charles Chaput of Philadelphia for reasserting the Catholic teaching that divorced and civilly remarried Catholics cannot receive Communion without abstaining from marital relations. Since then Farrell has become Francis's principal point man for the U.S. episcopate on *Amoris laetitia*.

58. Article 6 states, "Status as an Academician can be revoked pursuant to the Academy's own Regulations in the event of a

public and deliberate action or statement by a Member clearly contrary to the principles stated in paragraph b) above, or seriously offensive to the dignity and prestige of the Catholic Church or of the Academy itself."

The Declaration of the Servants of Life (no longer an "oath") required to be signed by all members, includes the stipulations, "3. The fertilized egg, the embryo, and the fetus may not be given away or sold. They may not be denied the right to progressive development in their mother's womb and may not be subjected to any kind of exploitation. 4. No authority, not even the father or the mother, may take the life of the unborn. A servant of Life may not perform actions such as destructive research on the embryo or fetus, elective abortion, or euthanasia."

59. Charlie Gard was born August 4, 2016 with a fatal genetic condition called mitochondrial DNA depletion syndrome. His parents wanted to take him to the United States to undergo experimental treatment at their own expense, but Great Ormond Street Hospital refused to release him saying the treatment would be of no benefit. The hospital also refused to allow the parents to take the child to die at home. Critics, many of them Catholic ethicists, said that this is a case of the state essentially imprisoning the child.

60. Michael Brendan Dougherty, "The Vatican's Statement on the Charlie Gard Case Is a Disgrace," *National Review*, June 30, 2017

61. Pope Francis, Twitter, @Pontifex, June 30, 2017.

62. Quoted in Claire Chretien, "Archbishop: Pope Told Me We Must Avoid Speaking 'Plainly' on Communion for Remarried," LifeSiteNews, May 9, 2016.

Chapter 5: Mercy! Mercy!

1. The original rule of the Franciscan order, approved in a Papal Bull in 1223.

2. Members of the order do take a fourth "Marian" vow in keeping with their charism in which they are specially consecrated to the Mother of God and pledge to work for the coming of Christ's kingdom in the world. Extra vows specific to an order's particular charism is normal in Catholic religious life.

3. The appetite for such Maria Monk fables of convent life appears never to have died among a certain class of readership. But their veracity is easily dismissed. As for "self-flagellation," the use of "the discipline"—a small bunch of cords made for the purpose and strictly regulated in a community's rules—was considered a normal penitential practice for all the centuries of the Church until Vatican II. The signing of vows in blood is absurd enough to simply ignore.

4. Another reason the Vatican had been reluctant to act was that the Legion made a great pretense of its orthodoxy and could indeed claim to have produced a number of good priests, something that endeared the Legion to Pope John Paul II.

5. An example of this, of which the Vatican took advantage, is given by the case of Monsignor de Bonis.

6. The title "Fra" indicates the knights professed of the three vows.

7. The cardinal patronus is the pope's diplomatic representative to the Order of Malta, while the Order names its own ambassador to the Holy See.

8. This and other parts of the papal letter were published by Riccardo Cascioli in *La Nuova Bussola Quotidiana*, February 2, 2017.

9. See Austen Ivereigh, *The Great Reformer*, 241.
10. These three noblemen may be inspected in a sadly comic photograph taken covertly in a Roman restaurant in January 2017, and published by the satirical website Dagospia (www.dagospia.com/rubrica-29/cronache/gran-papocchio-all-ordine-malta-gran-cancelliere-boeselager-ha-141049.htm), in which they are seen contemplating with marked lack of enthusiasm the catastrophe into which their resistance had plunged the Order.
11. Baron Boeselager from the beginning embarked on a policy of silencing criticism by intimidating sections of the media that pointed out the implausibilities in his version of events. Thus, he brought a lawsuit against the Austrian website Kath.net for quoting a critical article in *Bild*. (Curiously, he did not sue *Bild* itself.) In September 2017 his suit against Kath.net was dismissed by a court in Hamburg, which held that the grounds on which he had been dismissed by Grand Master Festing were to all appearance correct. Yet Boeselager remains in control of the Order of Malta and Festing remains deposed.

Chapter 6: Kremlin Santa Marta

1. Damian Thompson, "Why More and More Priests Can't Stand Pope Francis," *Spectator*, January 14, 2017.
2. The only person to raise the question of sexual misconduct was the archbishop of Asunción (Paraguay), who accused the priest, inaccurately, of having molested children. Bishop Livieres riposted by pointing out that the archbishop himself had been judicially investigated for homosexual acts.
3. Matthias Matussek in *Die Woche,* April 12, 2017.

4. Archbishop Becciu is a Sardinian, and it may be no coincidence that his hometown, Pattada, is famous for the production of knives.

5. Another whose name is rarely mentioned is Cardinal Mauro Piacenza, a Ratzingerian who had been prefect of the Clergy, where he had replaced Bergoglio's close collaborator the Brazilian liberal Cardinal Hummes. Immediately after Francis was elected, Piacenza, a noted "social conservative" was demoted to serve as Penitentiary Major.

6. Thompson, "Why More and More Priests."

7. It is worth recalling that, before deciding to enter the clerical state, Jorge Bergoglio worked as a nightclub bouncer in a Buenos Aires suburb. The experience seems to have been formative.

8. Lisa Bourne, "Pope Yet Again Derides Defenders of Church Teaching as Not Like Christ," LifeSiteNews, January 12, 2017. This provides the most authentic report of an anecdote which had been circulating for some weeks previously in Vatican circles.

9. The dismissal both of Cardinal Müller and of his subordinates fell short of the standards for the treatment of employees that should be observed in any ordinary company, let alone in a Church which preaches respect for workers' rights. The subject is treated by Damian Thompson in the *Spectator*, July 12, 2017: "Pope Francis Is Behaving Like a Latin American Dictator— but the Liberal Media Aren't Interested."

10. Sarah was transferred to the Congregation for Divine Worship from the Pontifical Council Cor Unum, where he had been charged by Pope Benedict with "re-catholicizing" the powerful and wealthy organization Caritas Internationalis that had been promoting leftist political causes. As president of Caritas

Internationalis, Pope Francis has installed Cardinal Tagle (whom many regard as his natural successor as the liberal *papabile* candidate) effectively halting Benedict's attempt at reform.

11. Maike Hickson, "Shakeup at Congregation for Divine Worship Described as a 'Purge,'" OnePeterFive, October 31, 2016.
12. Quoted in *Il Foglio*, November 29, 2016.
13. Voice of the Family, "Papal Critics Threatened with Excommunication as Year of Mercy Begins," LifeSiteNews, December 7, 2015.
14. Jan Bentz, "Some of 45 Signatories Feeling the Heat over Letter Urging Clarification of *Amoris Laetitia*," LifeSiteNews, September 29, 2016.
15. Sandro Magister in *L'Espresso*, November 14, 2016.
16. Philip Lawler, "The Ideological Purge at the Vatican," LifeSiteNews, January 26, 2017.
17. Nuzzi, *Merchants in the Temple*, 204.
18. Steve Skojec, "The Dictatorship of Mercy," OnePeterFive, November 17, 2016.
19. Thompson, "Why More and More Priests."
20. Ivereigh, *The Great Reformer*, 28.
21. Ibid., 383–84.
22. The two hundred posters were removed within hours by the city officials of Rome, where the pope has no legal jurisdiction. Posters advertising political opinions are known to remain on view in the city for years, undisturbed.
23. Valentina Conti, "E i fedeli manifestano la loro insoddisfazione disertando le udienze in piazza San Pietro," *Il Tempo*, July 2, 2017.
24. Quoted in Roberto de Mattei, "Papa Francesco quattro anni dopo," *Corrispondenza Romana*, March 15, 2017.

25. Philip Willan, "Anti-Reform Cardinals 'Want the Pope to Quit," *Times*, March 2, 2017; see also Damian Thompson, "The Plot against the Pope: It Is No Secret in Rome that Several Cardinals Want Francis to Stand Down," *Spectator*, March 11, 2017.

26. Antonio Socci in *Libero*, February 28, 2017.

27. Luigi Bisignani in *Il Tempo*, July 2, 2017, "Il Papocchio. La Solitudine di Papa Francesco. Dall' Argentina agli Stati Uniti cala la popolarità di Jorge Mario Bergoglio tra scandali, errori, epurazioni e faide interne che spaccano la Curia" ("The Papal Scam: The Loneliness of Pope Francis. From Argentina to the United States the popularity of Jorge Mario Bergoglio is falling, amid scandals, mistakes, purges and internal feuds splitting the Curia").

28. This story was first published by OnePeterFive on August 11, 2017, in the article by Alessandro Rico (a journalist on the Italian newspaper *La Verità*), "Democrat Fingers in the Vatican Pie: Did Obama Force Benedict's Abdication?" Independently of the details given in this article, it can be stated that the allegations rest on the word of two figures whose names have instant recognizability in the field of the Vatican's financial offices.

29. Bisignani, "Il Papocchio."

30. *Faithful Insight* (journal of LifeSiteNews), May 2017, quoting an article of Giuseppe Nardi in November 2016.

31. See Lucrecia Rego de Planas's *Letter to Pope Francis* quoted earlier. This peculiarity of the pope's is commented on in the epigram by Lorenzo Strecchetti: *Sono Francesco, papa ed argentino: / non all'Ostia, ma al secolo mi inchino*. Which might be translated: Francis, the Argentinian pope, that's me: / not to the Host but to the age I bend the knee. The verse comes

from a published collection of two hundred epigrams, *Francescheide,* subtitled *Pasquinate per papa Francesco*—another throwback to the disrespectful traditions of centuries ago which Francis has provoked.

32. Aldo Maria Valli, *266.* (Macerata: 2016), 186.

33. See, e.g., the report in *Libero Quotidiano,* December 21, 2017, "Papa Francesco, l'attacco alla Curia romana: l'accusa ai 'traditori.'"

34. See page 60.

35. See page 82.

36. John-Henry Westen, "Leaked Docs Raise Question of Pope's Personal Role in New Vatican Financial Scandal," LifeSiteNews, February 20, 2018.

37. In 1632 Urban VIII's refusal to support the Catholic cause in the face of the Protestant military victories that were sweeping over Europe caused Cardinal Ludovisi (the nephew of the previous pope) to threaten to depose him as a protector of heresy, while at one consistory Cardinal Borgia read out a formal protest, with the cardinals crowding round him to prevent the pope from silencing him. One of the pasquinades that appeared against Urban VIII asked, "Is His Holiness by chance a Catholic?"—a question which has been heard in our own times.

INDEX

D

Danneels, Godfried, 3–7, 9, 14–18, 46, 49, 71, 109
de Bonis, Donato, 55, 77
de Kirchner, Fernández, 157
de la Cigoña, Francisco José, 44
de Paolis, Velasio, 98, 152
de Paula, Ignacio Carrasco, 123
Devillé, Rik, 15
Dew, John, 109,
dicasteries, 58, 61–62, 81, 125, 174, 176
Dignitas personae, 108
Dolan, Timothy, 111
Donum vitae, 108, 123
Dougherty, Michael Brendan, 132
Doyle, Anne Barrett, 71
dubia, 119, 124, 166, 180

E

Egan, Edward, 39
Eijk, Willem,
El Verdadero Francisco (The Real Francis), 33
Erdo (cardinal), 103, 113-14, 185
Esterhazy, Janos, 154, 166
Estivill, Daniel Emilio, 39
Evangelii gaudium, 180, 192
Extraordinary Synod, 95, 98–99, 106, 108–9, 113

F

Familiaris consortio, 96, 116, 127, 129
Farrell, Kevin, 61–62

Fernández, Victor Manuel, 109
Festing, Matthew, 154–56, 160, 162–68
First Things, 20, 61
Fisichella, Rino, 121–23, 127, 179
Forte, Bruno, 66, 103, 109, 133
Francis (saint), 137, 139, 152
Franciscan Friars Minor, 151
Franciscan Friars of the Immaculate, 137–44, 146–48, 150–53, 168
Fürer, Ivo, 3, 6–7

G

Gabriele, Paolo, 56–57
Gadecki, Stanisław, 115, 118
García, Eduardo, 44
Gard, Charlie, 131–32
Geiger, Angelo M., 142
German Association, 154, 156, 166
Gli intoccabili, 57
Gormally, Luke, 127
Great Reformer, The, 18, 21
Grisez, Germain, 127
Grygiel, Stanislaw, 128
Grzegocki, Mieczyslaw, 127
Guardia de Hierro, 24, 28
Guardini, Romano, 31

H

Haari, Patrick, 64
Hart, Denis, 129
Henckel von Donnersmarck, Winfried, 154, 166
Hitchens, Dan, 129
Humanae vitae, 8, 10–11, 125
Hume, Basil, 6, 18

W

X

Y

Z